Youthful MEMORIES

Helen J. Bradberry

iUniverse, Inc.
New York Bloomington

Youthful Memories

iUniverse books may be ordered through booksellers or by contacting:

iUniverse
1663 Liberty Drive
Bloomington, IN 47403
www.iuniverse.com
1-800-Authors (1-800-288-4677)

Because of the dynamic nature of the Internet, any Web addresses or links contained in this book may have changed since publication and may no longer be valid. The views expressed in this work are solely those of the author and do not necessarily reflect the views of the publisher, and the publisher hereby disclaims any responsibility for them.

ISBN: 978-1-4502-5817-3 (sc)
ISBN: 978-1-4502-5818-0 (ebook)

Printed in the United States of America

iUniverse rev. date: 10/18/2010

Thank you, and foremost, to everyone who guided me in the writing of this book.

Extra-special thanks to my Sister-in-law Ann Zedlitz,
My daughter-in-law Jodi Bradberry,
My Son Steven Bradberry,
I could not have writing this book without you.

To my
Nearest and dearest sons:
Edwin David Bradberry,
Steven Duane Bradberry,

The Zedlitz Off-springs:
JW, Richard Edward, Ray G., Mary Jo, and Annie Ruth,

The Zedlitz Nieces and Nephew:
Lisa Gayl Fiedler,
Carol Denise Cootz,
Trishana Lynn,
Stacy Lee,
In Memory of Gerald Lee Purvis.

The Bradberry Grand Children:
Amber N., Travis Colter, Alena R., Corrie A., and Tristan Z.,

The Wise Grand Children:
Alison and Joseph,

The Great-Grand Children:
Madison Rose Heriford,
Janna Marie Florschuetz,
Terriance Moore,
Jesse Moore.

To any future Great-Grand-Children:

To my great-nephews:
Drifter Glen Vasser,
Colter Glen Vasser,

 I love you all.
Helen J.. Bradberry

Mark 10:27
And Jesus looking upon them saith, with men it is impossible, but not with God: for with God
all things are possible. I am writing my memories and the memories of other family members as
they were related to me. These memories are the first eighteen years of my life. I have added
historical facts that happened at different periods of my life. that I researched (1)).

1 in the New Standard Encyclopedia.

Table of Contents

CHAPTER

In 1939 or 1940: Dad had bought a John Deere steel wheel tractor to farm with. He was the first person to buy a tractor in Borden County in the State of Texas. Franklin Delano Roosevelt, a Democrat, was the President. The whole county was in a state of depression. The Japanese have bombed Pearl Harbor, December 7, 1941. The United States was in World War II. The times were very hard and would get harder.

Dad bought a 160 acres farm, 10 miles east of O'Donnell, in the fair state of Texas. The house had two rooms, no electricity, no running water and an outdoor toilet. A windmill was standing on the property that pumped water, when the wind blew. It stood two hundred feet from the house.

I, Helen Jean Zedlitz, was born March 23, 1942, to John William and Edna Clara Zedlitz. A neighbor, Mrs. Rains, was the midwife in attendance. Dad went to the nearest neighbor, who had a phone to call the doctor. Doctor Bubany did make it to the birthing on time.

I have three older brothers: JW, born July 18, 1931; Richard Edward, born June 10, 1937; and Ray G., born November 9, 1938.

I was six months old when Richard, Ray, and I had the Red Measles and Mumps. I don't know how Mom managed to take care of us three small children being sick, one right after the other during that time.

Mom had to take me and the three boy to the field when she was picking cotton. She would let me ride on the cotton sack. Ray picked piles of cotton just ahead of her, and Dad, and they picked up the cotton when they reached it. If Ray got tired, he would lay down and go to sleep on Dad's sack while he was working. Dad had to shake the cotton down in the sack, and Ray would fall off. That must have been in 1943, when I was a year old and Ray was four years old. Richard was five years old. He had his own gunny sack (toe sack) to pick cotton in.

Dwight D. Eisenhower was named Supreme Allied Commander in December, 1943. In this position he directed the cross-channel invasion of France that began June 6, 1944 and led to Germany's surrender in World War II.

Mary Jo was born July 14, 1944. The same midwife was in attendance. Dad went to a neighbor's house, who had a phone, called the same doctor, and he did not make it there on time. Mary Jo was born with her umbilical cord around her neck. Mrs. Rains was able to remove the umbilical cord from around Mary Jo's neck and she was fine. The doctor finally made it and he checked Mary Jo over and he told Mom, "the baby was alright."

President Franklin D. Roosevelt was reelected to be president, with Harry S. Truman of Missouri for Vice President. Roosevelt was president longer than any other man, having been elected to serve four terms.

Zedlitz family picture 1952

Richard Zedlitz age 12, 1947

Mary Jo Zedlitz age 9, 1950

John & Edna Zedlitz (mom & dad) 1965

CHAPTER 2

We moved later that year to Hagerman, New Mexico to a house with a porch. Someone gave us a puppy. Mary Jo was learning how to walk and we played with the puppy on the porch. She pulled the puppy's tail and the puppy bit her and Mom told Dad, "You have to get rid of the puppy." I never saw the puppy again. I learned years later that when Mom told Dad to get rid of a dog or cat, he killed it. Mom was expecting another baby.

President Roosevelt went to Warm Springs for a rest. On April 12, 1945, a portrait painter was making sketches of Roosevelt as he worked. The President slumped in his chair saying, "I have a terrible headache." He died a few hours later of cerebral hemorrhage. Within four hours Harry S. Truman took the oath of office as the thirty third President.

On May 8, 1945, President Truman proclaimed the unconditional surrender of Germany. The Allies issued a demand for Japan's surrender. When the Japanese ignored the ultimatum, President Truman ordered the use of a new and devastating weapon, the-atomic bomb. One was dropped on Hiroshima August 6, 1945 and a second on Nagasaki on August 9, 1945.

Mom went into labor and Annie Ruth was born on August 9, 1945, at home. A doctor was called and was in attendance. She was born inside of the placenta, which was called a veil. The doctor told Mom he had heard of babies being born inside a veil, but he had never seen it before. It was supposed to mean Annie would be clairvoyant, which she did turn out to be.

My brothers, Richard and Ray were baby setting me. They had to keep me outside. We were eating watermelon. Dad had Mary Jo in the house because she was only thirteen months old. JW

was working in the field, chopping cotton. After Annie was born, Dad called my brothers and I into the house to see our baby sister. My first glimpse of Annie was of a red, wrinkled, crying baby lying in Mom's arm.

Eisenhower held the highest rank possible for a United States officer-that of General of the Army. He commanded United States occupation forces in Germany.

On August 14, 1945, President Truman announced the surrender of Japan. Mom had three brothers fighting in the war over seas, and all three came home safely.

During that first year of Annie's life, Mom had breast cancer. She was operated on and the breast was removed. While Mom was recuperating, a Mrs. Kiper took care of Annie. Aunt Ella King took care of Mary Jo and me. The three boys, JW, Richard, and Ray stayed with Dad. I think JW had to take care of them. He was fourteen years old at that period of time.

JW got into trouble at school with two other boys. They were caught smoking off the school ground. They all received a whipping in front of their class. JW was embarrassed and mad so he quit school. I could not ever remembered him going to school. He never totally quit smoking either.

Aunt Ella kept Mary Jo & me while Mom had her surgery. She gave Mary Jo a bath in a dish pan. I was too big, so she gave me a bath in a # 2 wash tub. She let us eat crackers in bed at night. The ants would bite me as I slept. I would have bite marks that were red and itchy the next day. She would make me stay out side and play while Mary Jo would be taking a nap. She was 18 months old, so she was still just a baby.

After Mom spent two weeks in the hospital from her surgery, we went back home. Mom had to take care of Mary Jo, Mrs. Kiper was keeping Annie and taking care of her. I was 3 ½ years old, Mary Jo was 1 ½ years old, Ray was 6 years old, Richard was 7 years old, and JW was 15 years old. JW and Richard had to help Mom a lot. Richard would have to keep an eye on us when JW was in the field working. I know they resented us little ones. They would tease and torment us every chance they got.

I could understand why: Richard never had time to play cowboy and Indians or Roy Rogers and Gene Artery. He and Ray would play when ever they could and when I wasn't pestering them.

Mary Jo was going through the terrible twos. I would have to help Mom with Mary Jo and try to keep her from getting into trouble most of the time.

That year the whole family took a trip back to O'Donnell, Texas. My favorite Uncle Henry died. He was Dad's younger brother. We were at the funeral home. Dad told me, "Uncle Henry was asleep." Dad lifted me up to see him lying in an open coffin. I ask Dad, "Why did Uncle Henry sleep with his clothes and shoes on and not in his own bed?" If he gave me an answer I do not remember it. I do not remember going to the cemetery after the funeral.

We went back to New Mexico after the funeral. Dad moved us from Hagerman to Las Cruces, New Mexico. The house was very large with a screened back porch, a bath room, running water and electricity. It was like a hacienda. There were morning glory flowers every where around the house and in the fields. Mary Jo and I played in the back yard. The area that stayed wet and turned black and stunk like rotten mud was were the cesspool was. Mary Jo would play in the stinky mud and eat it. She would have a fit if you made her stop playing in it. I would go tell Mom, she would bring her in the house, and clean Mary Jo up, and she would be screaming at the top of her lungs. JW and other Mexican workers chopped the morning glories out of the fields or someone would have to plow the fields to remove the flowers.

While we lived in Las Cruces and Mom was still recovering from the surgery. She took my sisters and I to O'Donnell to see Grandma. We must have gone by bus. She lived at the edge of town. We had to sleep on the floor on pallets. I had to play outside with my cousins, Carol and John. Grandma and Aunt Lois were keeping them since their Dad had died. He had been working on his car and the engine fell on him and crushed him. Aunt Maudie, their mother, was working as a telephone operator in O'Donnell. Aunt Lois made us stay outside to play. I got sick and she did not believe me until I threw up in front of her. Then she let me come in and lay down. I was sick all that day. Somebody bought sodas and I was given an orange one, which I could not keep down. I only remember Mom being around that day later in the afternoon. I don't know where she was all day. I thought she might have gone to see another doctor for a second opinion. I cannot recall how long we stayed, or when we left there.

Annie Zedlitz age 12, 1957

JW & Betty Zedlitz, 1960

CHAPTER 3

Dad moved us to Arizona in a 1937 steel bed International truck, green and black in color. Dad would tell us it had a grandma gear for climbing hills. We moved half way between Tempe and Mesa. Dad worked on the Haines Farm, irrigating vegetables and cotton. There was a Pima Indian reservation close by. Dad worked with the Indians. The Indians paid Dad 25 cents each to ride to town on Saturdays to get groceries or to the field to work.

On Saturdays my family would go to town to buy groceries. All of us children would ride in the back of the truck with the Indians except Annie, who was a baby. Sometimes JW would have to drive us. Mom would complain about the Indians riding in the truck with us children. Dad had to work that particular Saturday. JW drove us all to town to buy groceries including the Indians. When it was time to go back to the camp the Indians would not pay JW the 25 cents each. There were about 15 Indians. He left them at the store. JW stopped to put gas in the truck, which was across the road from the store.

The gas tank was under the passenger seat. The gas station attendant spilled some gas. The battery was under the floor on the driver's side and some of the spilled gas ran into the battery, which caused a spark on the battery cables and started a fire. Mom was setting right on top of the gas tank. JW had pulled out on the road and was headed to camp. I looked up and the cab was full of flames and Mom was screaming. Mom threw Annie out the window on the side of the road. Annie was not hurt. JW had to crawl out on the passenger side so he must have helped Mom out of the truck. He was hollering to get out of the back of the truck before the truck exploded. If he had not filled up the truck tank it would have exploded. JW and the boys threw dirt on the flames

until the fire department got there. Somebody took Mom to the doctor. I cannot recall who. I went to the doctor with her. She had burns on her hands, arms, and legs. I know he put some kind of salve on her burns. She wasn't burned too badly. She was not put in a hospital. While the truck was burning, the Indians were still across the road at the grocery store. They did not even come over to help put out the fire. They were jumping up and down, laughing their heads off. I guess they believed Mom got what she deserved for complaining about them riding in the back of the truck and JW got what he deserved for not letting them ride for free.

It was 1946. Dad had to pay $300.00 to have all the wiring replaced in the truck, to replace the windshield, and the back window. That old 1937 International steel bed truck was all we had to ride in.

One place we lived was on Eloy Farms around Eloy, Arizona in a workers' camp. The cabins were one room made of adobe. We had three different rooms, one for the kitchen, and two rooms for the bedrooms. The owner of the Eloy Farm gave the workers and their families an ice cream party. They brought the ice cream to us in gallon cartons of strawberry, vanilla, and chocolate. The strawberry ice cream was so good; it was my favorite. The watermelon was sun ripen and picked out of the field. We did not have the watermelon and ice cream to eat at the same time.

A couple of old men working in the camp were drunks. Richard asked Dad one day, "Way do those two men buy booze when they could have ice cream and watermelon?" Dad answered back, "I don't understand, either, why someone would give up ice cream and watermelon for booze." While we lived there, I was bit by an insect. Mom took me on the bus to Phoenix to see a doctor. I had a large purple boil on my face. The doctor lanced the purple boil and put some medicine on it. He was teasing me saying he was putting monkey blood on my face. I answered him back saying I did not want any monkey blood on my face. We rode the bus back to Eloy and the camp. Of course I had a big story to tell about the bus rides and the doctor putting monkey blood on my face.

During that summer of 1946, Mom, Richard, Ray, and JW chopped cotton. Dad was still irrigating and working with the Indians. Richard chopped cotton in the mornings and Mom would cook dinner. She would go to the field and chop cotton in the afternoon and Richard would baby sit Annie. Mom took Mary Jo and me to the field with her. We would play on the row she was working on, either just ahead of her or at the end of the row. My job was to make sure Mary Jo stayed with me; We had to stay where Mom could see us. I was four years old taking care of a two year old. Richard and Annie were back at the camp taking a nap that particular afternoon. Richard woke up and saw a coiled rattle snake lying between Annie and him. He laid real still, without moving, until the snake moved off the bed. The snake slithered off the bed and went through a mouse hole in the wall.

The men in the camp burned the grass around the camp that afternoon. A snake was found burned in a large can, which somebody had thrown out into the grass. We never did know if it was the same snake. Usually if you see one snake there will be a another snake close by or even a den of snakes. Mom and Dad did not intend to stay around long enough to see if there were more snakes to contend with.

CHAPTER 4

The day after the snake incident Mom and Dad decided to move back to Texas. We left Arizona and stopped in New Mexico to see Uncle Paul and Aunt Ella. Uncle Paul talked Dad in to staying and working for him. He had a three room shack on his place, so we moved into it. The shack was really dirty with a lot of trash that had to be burned. There was no electricity in the house though it did have running water. There was a deep ditch (canal) running in front of the house. There was no water running down the ditch (canal) at that time. It must have been the fall of 1947. I had not started to school yet.

Mom was still recuperating from her cancer surgery. When we went to town on Saturdays, Dad would do the laundry. Mom helped him by sorting the clothes into piles. There were usually five or six piles of clothes, sorted in the order of whites, sheets, towels, dress clothes and colored clothes. The laundry had rows and rows of ringer washers. Dad washed the clothes in separate washers for each load of clothes. There was nothing automatic in that laundry. He washed each load about 30 minutes.

Dad would give us children pennies and we would raid the peanut machine while he was doing the laundry. We would get a hand full of peanuts and a small toy about an inch long with one penny. I would collect the little toys and put them on a string. I had seen a truck that had a full string of the little plastic toys hanging across the dash. Mom would also buy cracker jacks, which had the small toys in each box. Mary Jo and I would play with the little toys for hours. I don't know what the boys did while Dad was doing laundry, probably played hide and seek or cowboys and Indians outside.

Dad ran the clothes through the ringer into the first rinse tub, then the second tub, and then into a tub to take the clothes home in. He did the same thing for each of the five or six full washers. He had two or three wash tubs to carry the washed clothes home in to hang out on the clothes line to dry. Dad or the boys must have hung the clothes out to dry once we got home. I was still to small to reach the cloth line.

Mom would do her own laundry, washing her underclothes on a rub board. She would rub them on a rub board until they were show white. She washed her clothes that way as long as she was able to.

The boys had to pick cotton that fall. They bought a red wagon with their money for Christmas that year. We had a lot of fun with that wagon. Then they bought a bicycle and learned how to ride. It was too big for us girls. We didn't attempting to ride it for a few years.

The boys had to walk a mile to catch the bus. They went to school at East Grand Plains. They wore overalls to school; they did not have any jeans to wear. Some of the other boys would laugh and make fun of them and bully Ray into fighting with them. Richard would have to come to Ray's rescue more than once when he was being bullied by three of the Mexicans. Richard had a class next door to Ray's class. Richard would hear someone getting a whipping every day in Ray's class. Richard figured it was Ray. It was Ray; he remembered getting a whipping every day for aggravating other students, the teacher, and not doing his lessons. Ray must have been in the second grade.

The shack we lived in on Uncle Paul's farm had a window box made of wood and chicken wire, right outside of the kitchen window. Mom would put cheese, milk and some meat in the window box in the winter time. We had an ice box, which you would have to buy block ice for from the ice house once a week. She would also put left over food in it. One night Uncle Paul's dog tore the window box up to get to the food. That was the end of the window box.

One morning I was following Dad as he walked in front of Aunt Ella's house. He was going to see Uncle Paul and I wanted to see Aunt Ella. The dog did not move when Dad walked by. I was walking about ten feet behind him and the dog raised up and started after me. I started running and screaming and the dog bit me on my bottom. Dad had to get the dog off of me. That was one dog bite that I never forgot. Aunt Ella cleaned me up and put some medicine on the dog bite. I kept my distance and never got close to that dog again. I never heard if the dog bit any one else. They kept the dog and never tied him up.

It was the spring of 1948. Dad planted cotton and watermelons that had to be irrigated. The deep ditch or canal had water running down it being pumped out of a well. It was deep enough to be over the top of my head when it was full of water. There was only a plank for us to walk across to get to the other side. The road leading to the house was over there and Dad parked his 1937 International steel bed truck over there.

An accident happen that summer that I will never forget. One morning Mary Jo and I were playing outside and I walked across the plank to get to the other side. Mary Jo tried to do every thing I would do. She was three years old and I was five years old.

She went prancing across the plank and started back across the plank. She fell into the ditch full of water. I saw her fall and run across the plank screaming, "Mom," without falling in myself. Mom came running to see what was the matter and saw Mary Jo sitting in the bottom of the ditch playing. She got into the ditch and pulled Mary Jo out of the water. When Mom pulled Mary Jo out of the water, she was sitting in a bubble, still breathing air, and under no stress at all. Mary Jo even told Mom, " I was in a bubble." You can call it what ever you want, but a miracle happened that day, and the good Lord was with her. The water in the ditch was flowing; it could have carried her on down the ditch before Mom could have got to her.

It was September of 1948. I should have started school. The boys were picking cotton. They could not start school until the cotton was picked. Mom wouldn't let me walk the mile to catch the bus alone. I had to wait until the boys started to school.

Dwight D. Eisenhower, Army Chief of Staff, retired from the Army in 1948. Eisenhower was a very important military man in World War II. He would soon be a very important person in the United States.

Mary Jo and I picked cotton on the end of Mom and Dad's rows. We made big piles of cotton. They were picking and putting the cotton in 10 to 12 foot sacks. Mom and Dad picked up the piles of cotton that we had picked and put it into their sacks. When the cotton sacks were full, Dad threw the full sack over his shoulder and carried it to the scales to weigh the cotton. The cotton could weigh up to 80 pounds or more. The cotton was then dumped into a trailer. When the trailer was full, it would be taken to the cotton gin and baled.

JW bought a Victrola record player that ran off a battery, which you had to crank with a handle, with the money he made picking cotton. He also bought some records. The one we played the most was "Eddy Arnold and the Cattle Call." We would play that record over and over. " How Much is that Doggy in the Window." Was one of the records that we liked. I think it was sung by Patty Page. Another record was "Open the Door Richard." I do not know who sang that song.

Harry S. Truman ran for election and was elected President of the United States in 1948.

Another accident happened that same year. Dad still had the 1937 International steel bed truck. The sideboards were not on the truck, except in the back of the cab, which we used to hold on to when the truck was moving. Richard, Ray, Mary Jo and I were riding in the back of the truck. JW was driving and Mom and Annie were in the cab. Mary Jo was sitting next to me when JW turned left as we arrived in town. She started to slide. Richard, Ray, and I were hanging on to the sideboard with both hands. She kept on sliding and slid right off the back of the truck and landed in the middle of the road. A car was coming and was able to stop. Richard got JW's attention and he pulled over to the side of the road and stopped. JW ran back and picked up Mary Jo. She was crying but not hurt. This time he put her in the cab. I do not under understand why Mom let a three year old ride in the back of a truck with no sideboards to hold on to. It was hard enough for me to hang on with both hands, without having a small child to help hang on too. Mom expected me to take care of Mary Jo. Mom was too careless with us children, placing us in life threatening incidents.

We were still living on Uncle Paul's farm in the same shack. Dad sent Richard to ask Uncle Paul

for something. He knocked on the door and Uncle Paul came to the door. When Richard saw him standing at the door, he forgot what he was suppose to ask him. Uncle Paul immediately accused Richard of stealing watermelons. Richard denied it, telling him he was only in the watermelon field when Dad was. He told Richard, "If I ever catch you stealing my watermelons, I will shoot you." He told Richard , "I shot at you before." Richard told him, "You never shot at me before." Richard found out later from a neighbor boy that Uncle Paul had shot at him when he was stealing watermelons.

Ray and I were out in the watermelon field one day busting melons and eating only the heart. That might have triggered Uncle Paul's wrath, watching the melon field with a gun, and actually shooting at anybody he saw. We stayed out of the melon field after that. If we got a watermelon, Dad would have to bring it home.

Richard, Ray, and I finally started to school at East Grand Plains in the fall of 1948. I was six years old. We walked a mile to catch the bus to go to school. It had to be in October or November because it was very cold. My hands and feet would get so cold that I could not feel them.

Mom bought us long handled underwear to keep warm. I would push the long sleeves up under the sleeves of my dress, when I took off my coat. The boys laughed and made fun of me whenever they saw me with my arms covered with the underwear. I also had to wear ugly brown stockings to cover my legs. Little girls did not wear pants back then. I had a long coat to wear. I never had a sweater or sweat shirt to wear and neither did the boys.

My teacher was an elderly white hair lady. She was a good teacher. She tried to teach me how to read out of the Dick and Jane primer. I was so far behind the class I couldn't catch up. I couldn't read but a few words and I couldn't print my name. Zedlitz was not a easy name to learn to write. I knew the alphabet, but I didn't know the letters or how to write them. I did not get any help at home. If I asked Mom she would say, "I cannot see the words." I did not keep count of how many times she told me that through the years. I found out years later that she could not read or write. She could sign her name though. The boys couldn't help me, they were struggling to catch up with their own lessons.

We had lunch in the cafeteria. We had a choice of orange juice or milk to drink with our lunch. The milk was goat's milk, and I sure did not like it. The orange juice was probably powdered added to water, like Tang. I chose the orange juice to drink.

There was a small store across the road from the school. It was a few weeks before Christmas. The store sold suckers on a stick in the shape of Santa Clauses and Christmas trees. I wanted one so bad. I didn't have a nickel to buy one. Sometimes Dad would give me a penny or two. I finally did get to buy three suckers before Christmas. I took them home to share with Mary Jo and Annie. The suckers were a real treat for the three of us.

The first grade exchanged names for Christmas. I drew a boy's name. The gift that Mom bought for me to take to school was a rubber gun and a Christmas card. She did not even wrap the gift. I was so ashamed. I didn't even take it to school. I told the teacher I forgot to bring it to school. The gift I received was a nice gift. It was a purse with a shoulder strap I could carry on my shoulder. It was the only purse I would receive until I was nine years old. I would have to buy it myself.

Mary Jo had another accident. Since we didn't have electricity, Mom ironed clothes with cast irons that you had to heated on a stove. Mom used a square table to iron on. She sat in a chair while she ironed clothes. Mary Jo was running around playing. She bumped the table and knocked the iron off on her bare foot. Amazingly, she didn't break her foot. Mom did have vinegar, water, and soda to soak her foot in. The tip of the iron seared her foot showing the imprint of the iron. She did not get a scar from the burn.

Richard Zedlitz at New Moore, Texas 1949

Mary Jo Zedlitz age 15, 1959

Helen J. Bradberry

Uncle Lloyd McDaniel and
Grandma McDaniel 1945

CHAPTER 5

We moved to New Moore, Texas after Christmas that year. The New Year rang in and it was 1949. Dad farmed for a farmer, a Mr. Singleton, who had a worker's camp. We lived in a four room house. It did have running water and electricity. There was also an out door toilet that every one in the camp had to use. There were one room cabins that the Mexicans lived in.

When we lived at New Moore my first memory of Uncle Daniel was when he came to live with us. He was retarded. He would move around the country living with his brothers and sisters until they ran him off or he decided to move on. He would live with Aunt Ella a while then move on and live with Uncle Otto and his family a while. It was our turn, so he came to live with us. He had four more sisters in East Texas that he would live with. He would tell us of riding the rails and living as a hobo. He would work with Dad chopping cotton or picking cotton. He would pick up things as he walked and keep them. He had a trunk that he kept the things that he picked up in, which was off limits to us children. One day I got nosy and looked in his trunk. It was a child's paradise; he had pretty colored marbles and all kind of things that a child would like. I took some of the things out of his trunk and he found out and got mad. I had to give them back and stay out of his trunk. He started locking the trunk after that.

The school we went to was New Moore. It was a red brick building that had a second floor. The school had first through the eight grades. First grade was on the first floor in the same room with the second and third grades.

First grade was reading out of the Dick and Jane primer in Texas also. I failed the first grade that year and I had to repeat the first grade. During the second year the first, second and third grades' children were in a play. The play was called the Old Woman in a shoe, which came from a nursery rhyme. The teacher dressed me up as the old woman. I wore a long dress and I was padded to look plump. My long dark hair was put up on top of my head and filled with corn starch to look like I had gray hair. I had to wear granny classes, which had no glass in them. I must have looked the part because the teacher kept me as the old lady. I did not know why the teacher picked me to be the old woman, unless it was because I was taller than the other children. The rest of the children had different parts. The PTA and all the parents came to see this play. They had a good laugh at the children acting out the play.

Mom and Dad went to O'Donnell to buy groceries, from Mansels' Grocery Store, which was owned by two brothers. The brothers would put a bag of candy (lemon drops, candy corn, gum drops or jelly beans) in the basket for us children each week. We thought they were giving us the candy, but they were adding the candy to the grocery bill. The bag of candy probably cost fifteen cents if that much. Dad discovered what they were doing and quit trading there and went to the R and W Grocery Store. The store had a red and white sign with R and W on it.

Occasionally, we would get a soda for a nickel, then it went up to six cents. We would get the RC Cola because it was in a bigger bottle. It was a real treat to get a Baby Ruth candy bar since it was twice as big for ten cents.

We were still living at New Moore when my sisters and I had the Whopping Cough. We had to be quarantine to stay away from other children. Richard and Ray didn't get it, I don't know why. We had a hard time being sick with the high fever and coughing every breath. We had to stay in a room with a vaporizer going 24 hours a day. We were taking some nasty tasting medicine and had to have black drops that we had to keep in our mouth like cough drops. Even after all the medicine we had to take, we still coughed every breath. Mary Jo had it the worst. She had to sleep in a tent with the vaporizer and her fever raged out of control at night. Mom had to keep a constant vigil with her. She would start choking when she would cough. Mom had trouble giving her the medicine without her choking and got Dad to help her. Mary refused to take the horse pills, they were that large. Mom had to mash the pills into a powder and put the medicine into oatmeal or mashed potatoes to get her to take it. The cough lasted about three months and finally faded away.

We had a dog named Buster. I do not know what kind of dog he was. He was just a large dog with a red and white coat. We would ride a bus to school and he would meet the bus every day. One day JW dressed him up in a shirt and pants and let him loose to meet the bus. My brothers and I were riding the school bus. Everyone on the bus laughed when they saw Buster.

Uncle Otto and Aunt Lizzy Zedlitz have eight children. Each one was close to my family in age. We all got along and played together very well. They were living on Dad's farm south east of O'Donnell in Borden County. We visited back and forth on Sundays. Mom would fry chicken and make banana pudding for dinner, when they came to visit. We would go see them the next Sunday and Aunt Lizzy would fry chicken and make banana pudding. One time she did make a cobbler pie out of tomatoes. I sure did not like the tomato cobbler and I cannot stand fried chicken and banana pudding until this day.

My second year at New Moore I was in the same room with Ray. I was still in the first grade and Ray was in the third grade. Every morning the teacher would call the roll. Each student's name was called and would answer, "I." One morning I was being stubborn. She called my name and I did not answer. She looked up and saw me and called my name again. I still didn't answer. I could see that she was getting upset and the other children in the class were trying to get me to answer her. She looked at Ray and told him to tell me to answer. Ray told me, "if you don't answer, I am going to tell Dad and you know what he will do to you." I was afraid of Dad. I had seen him whip the boys more than once with a razor strap, which was a leather belt.

Mom would always threaten us by saying, "I will tell your Dad when he gets home if you don't behave." When the teacher called my name again I answered, "I." She continued calling the roll and I never did that again.

I had all day at school to think about what I had done that morning and worrying about Ray telling Dad. When we were going home after school I begged Ray not to tell Dad. If he did, Dad never said anything to me about my actions at school that day.

That summer we played outside until dark. We played hide and seek or tag. It was starting to get dark and a full moon was coming up. Richard saw the full moon and he and Ray were talking about it. Richard said, "that full moon means someone has died." I was listening, big eyed, and believing every word he said. Later that same night, Ray told me if you promise to do something and don't do it, you will die. I was guilty of promising somebody something and not doing it. I was totally convinced that since there was a full moon, and I was guilty of promising to do something and hadn't done it, I was going to die if I went to sleep.

Later that night I had trouble going to sleep. I was afraid I was going to die. I was only seven years old and I sure did not want to die. It must have been around midnight. I woke up Dad and ask him, "if the full moon meant someone had died and if you promised to do something and didn't do it you would die?" He told me, "no," and he ask me, "Who in the world told you something like that?" I answered him saying, "Richard and Ray told me." He told me, "You go back to bed, go to sleep and you will be all right." That was the best news I had heard all evening. I felt the weight of the world lift off my shoulders. I was more afraid of dying than I was afraid of waking Dad up. He did not get mad at me. I guess he saw that I was scared to death.

The boys were always doing or saying something that would scare us. We were so gullible that we believed everything anyone told us. They would make us walk into a dark room and back telling us the boogie man was in there. We would do it, just to prove we could, but our skinny little legs would be trembling. I was afraid of a dark room or house and Mom would leave a night light on in the bed room all of my growing up years.

The boys would get us down and tickle us. We would scream bloody murder and Mom never came to our rescue one time. I finally had to psyche my mind out and think that it did not tickle. If we did not scream and holler, they would leave us alone; it wasn't fun any more. Why Mom let the boys torment us girls, I will never know. I have never been able to scream again and I have always wandered why. If I try to scream my throat freezes up and all I can get out is a groan or a squeak.

Mary Jo was 4 years old, a live wire who needed to be controlled by an adult instead of by me, a seven year old.

She would go into the Mexicans' cabin next to us while they were at work. She took a plastic what-not, that looked like a toy, of a donkey bobbing its head and pulling a cart. She took it home and was playing with it. Mom was totally oblivious of what Mary Jo was doing.

When the Mexican lady got home and found it missing, she immediately came over angry and yelling at Mom. Mom made Mary Jo give it back to her.

One day on the way home from the field, Richard notice bugs crawling in one of the Mexican's hair that was riding with them. He told Mom and she and Dad checked all of our hair and we all had lice. She got mad and went out to the Mexicans cabin and cussed them out. We all had to have our hair washed in kerosene and water to kill the lice.

Ray Zedlitz, New Moore, Texas 1949

CHAPTER 6

We had to move again after Mom had a fight with the Mexicans over Mary Jo going into their cabin and taking something and Mom fighting with them over giving us lice. The day we moved the Mexicans were working in the field. The lady came in early to fix lunch. The lady came to me saying, " I want my donkey and cart back."   I told her, I did not have it, had not seen it, and did not know where it could be.   When we fully moved to the old home place, I realized that Mary Jo must have taken the donkey and cart and hid it.   Mary Jo brought the donkey out and played with it.   Then it was too late to give it back to the Mexican lady.

Uncle Otto and his family moved from Dad's farm to another small town.
We move back home to Borden County to Dad's 160 acres farm. Uncle Otto had built three rooms on the two room house. We now had a five room house with no electricity and no running water. Water had to be carried into the house from the windmill which was about 200 feet from the house.

Cousin Fred stayed a couple weeks with us after Uncle Otto and Aunt Lizzy moved.   He was working for REA out of O'Donnell. Mom would fix him a lunch every day which he took to work in a lunch bucket.   That same lunch bucket was kept on the floor in the kitchen when he was not using it.   One day he stopped coming back to the house and Mom was no longer making lunches for him.   I ask her why he was not coming to stay with us anymore and she said, " I don't know."

One Sunday we went up to see Uncle Otto and Aunt Lizzy to see where they lived.   They had moved 30 miles from O'Donnell.   They had gone to church and were not there so we waited until they got home.   Just as soon as Aunt Lizzy got home, she jumped on Mom and was really telling her off. I heard Aunt Lizzy say something about nasty children.   Mom answered her back,

"Your own nasty children did it." We left and went back home and Mom was crying and would not tell us what had happened. She never would go back to see them again. When Dad went he would take us children with him. We wondered what could have happened for years.

It must have been in the fall of 1949 when we made this move. Richard, Ray, and I would be going to school at Berry Flat in a two room school house with four grades in each room. The rooms were called the little room and the big room. There was a folding petition that separated the two rooms. The school was about a mile north of the house and we rode the bus to school every day.

The boys must have been picking cotton. I walked the mile to school my first day alone. It was very cold and I was wearing a dirty blue coat. My hair was wind blown and looked like I hadn't combed it. My nose and cheeks were red from the cold. I was carrying a red lord bucket with my lunch in it. I must have looked like a homeless orphan.

The teacher was Mrs. Wade and her husband drove the school bus. She welcomed me into the class room and I was the only one in the first grade for a while. She taught me how to read out of the Dick and Jane primer. She had more time to spend with me one on one, since I was the only first grader. I memorized the Dick and Jane Primer. I had been reading it for two years. I passed to the second grade and made good grades.

After I learned to read, I loved reading. My favorite book was <u>Tom Sawyer</u> and <u>Huckleberry Finn</u> I read all the <u>Canterbury Tales</u> and the <u>Wizard of Oz</u>. I loved reading the nursery rhymes and there was a book called <u>Little Black Sambo</u> I enjoyed. I cannot recall all the books I read.

Mary Jo and Annie had the Red Measles. Mary Jo had the measles first. She had a high fever, broke out with itchy red spots, and had to stay in a dark bedroom. The light hurt her eyes. Once she started feeling better, she was a holly terror to keep in the dark room. When I came home from school I had to stay in there and play with her. Mom didn't have to worry about me getting the measles because I had them when I was a baby. A side effect from the measles was Mary Jo had a lot of ear aches for the next three years. Annie got the Red Measles next. She was just as sick with a high fever, broke out with the itchy red spots, and had to stay in a dark bedroom. She wasn't as much trouble keeping in the dark bedroom. The light hurt her eyes too bad. After she recovered, she had to wear glasses. The doctor told Mom the Measles had settled in her eyes.

Mary Jo started to school in 1950. Both of us are in the same room. You had to raise your hand to be excused to go outside to the toilet or get a drink of water. We had a different teacher and she was old and mean. We were all afraid of her. She loved to whip a student in front of the whole class if he was misbehaving. She kept a whipping paddle on her desk at all times.

When we had an art class at Berry Flat, the teacher made copies of pages from a coloring book for us children to color. The copier was a tray about 12 inches by 18 inches long, filled with a firm jelly like substance. She put ink in this substance, made the copies one at a time of the same picture. Some times she would let one of us students make the copies.

We went to see Grandma often. She would always have fried salt pork and biscuits left over in the oven. I would go to the oven every time and get a biscuit and fried salt bacon and eat it. She

cooked a lot of butter beans and made grape cool-aid for dinner, which was lunch, Mary Jo would always ask for seconds in butter beans and grape cool-aid. Grandpa started calling her more butter beans. Sometimes Dad would send us over to Grandma, we would be out of the way when the butchering of the hog took place.

Once a year Dad would butcher a hog. It must have been on a week end because it seemed I was always there unless Dad sent Mary Jo and I to Grandma's house. The weather was always cold. It must have been in the winter just before spring.

Dad boiled water in a cast iron pot outside. He must have used wood but I don't know where he would have gotten any wood since there was no trees on the property. The actual killing I could not watch. Dad shot the hog between the eyes, then he slit his throat to let him bleed. The hog was making so much noise I through he was screaming. I went and hid my head and covered my ears; I could not stand it. Once the hog was dead, Dad put the boiling water on him and scraped all the hair off of the hog's body. He then hoisted the hog up and let him hang so the blood would drip out of the body. Dad cut him open from the chest to the hind legs. He removed all the intestines and the organs. You could see the ribs and back bone inside the cavity. The only organ that he kept was the liver. I don't know if he buried the rest of the organs or gave them away. Dad proceeded to cut up the hog into ribs, roast, hams, and bacon and the meat he ground up for sausage. For the first killing, we did not have electricity.

Dad salted the meat down with a special sugar curing salt and placed the meat in the smoke house. The meat could be kept for months. Mom would have to cook up the liver and the ribs right away. We only had an ice box which you had to buy block ice for weekly from the ice house. It would not freeze the liver or ribs. We always had pig liver and ribs for dinner after the slaughter of the hog. Mom would fry the liver and bake the ribs in the oven. I do not believe she ever barbecued the ribs. We didn't know the difference any way. We had never eaten barbecued ribs. The fat he rendered down in the cast iron pot outside and cracklings was made and the grease made lard. Dad finally contacted REA, Rural Electric Association, that summer, and Cousin Fred an electrician connected the electricity to the house after the high line poles were placed on the property and the lines were run. We had electricity on the old home place, and that was a day to remember. Now we could use Mom's refrigerator and deep freezer, instead of the ice box that you had to buy block ice for every week.

There was a drought going on and the country had received very little rain the past two years. The sand storms had been blowing and they were terrible. We are at school and school had to send everyone home on the bus. The sand was blowing so hard, you could not see a foot in front of you, like fog but worse. No one should have been driving in it. The sand filters into the house covering everything. I had to sweep buckets of sand out of the house. It covered the bed coverings, got in your hair, and on your face. It was like a mud pack on your face except the sand was dry. The storms would last for two to three days sometimes. Mom had trouble keeping the sand out of the food she cooked. She put lids on the pots while cooking. When you put the food on your plate the sand would filter into the food.

When we were able to go back to school, every student would have to help clean up the school room before starting class. There was no janitor working at Berry Flat. More than once I would take a broom and sweep out the class room. That was my job at home, before I even caught the bus to go to school. I would have to make up beds and sweep the front room before going to school every day.

The front room was being wall papered. Dad was putting black tar paper on chicken wire and stuccoed the outside of the house. He never painted the house. The house was warmer and looked better.

The Cokes are now ten cents. It was still a treat to be able to get one. We still like the RC Colas and would buy one whenever we had a dime.

Ray Zedlitz with friend, New Moore, Texas

Mom, Helen Zedlitz with cousins Florence and Janice Zedlitz

CHAPTER 7

I was about 8 years old when Grandma McDaniel had a nervous break down. At least that was what the doctor called it. She was sure acting strange. She was always looking for her nose. I am not kidding. She would say, "somebody took my nose." Aunt Lois would tell her, "Go look under your pillow, that is where you will find it." Grandma would argue about it, "No, it will not be under my pillow because somebody took it." I often wondered what she thought somebody would want with her nose.

The other strange thing she was doing was rolling up her dress tail to her crotch. She did that everywhere she went. Aunt Lois told the doctor about what she was doing and he told her, "She needs to do something with her hands, get her some pencils and tablets so she can doodle on them." Aunt Lois got her some Big Chief tablets and pencils, that first graders used, and gave them to her. It worked. She quit rolling up her skirt tail and started marking up the tablets. She did that for years until she died.

One Saturday, Mom let me go to see Peggy Burnett, she lived next door to the Berry Flat School and a mile from the house. I took the shortcut through the cow pasture. I stayed a couple of hours until Peggy's Mother told me, "It was time for me to go home my husband will be home soon." I left walking through a field on the side of their house. I walked through a dump that had tin cans full of dirt and paper. I found a rubber ball with a big hole in it full of dirt. It had a face on the ball which looked like the man in the moon. I kicked it and it rolled, so I kicked it again and kicked it all the way home. I never touched the ball after that to play with. I could have kicked a can and had as much fun with it.

That Monday when I went to school. Peggy and everyone in the class were standing beside her talking and she approached me. She said, "My Mom saw you take a ball, that had a face on it, a hole in the side, and I want it back." I told her, "Yes, it was in the dump where I thought you had throw it away, and I will bring it back." She branded me as a thief and I was so embarrassed I could have died on the spot. Needless to say, I have never went through anyone's dump again. The next day I brought the ball with me to school, I took it over to her house, and I threw it into her yard. She ask me when she saw me, "Did you bring the ball back," and I answered her saying, "Yes, and I threw it into your yard right where you could see it." That ball lay in the same place for the next year. I never went to see her again.

It was recess and Mary Jo was in the first grade. She and four of her class mates were playing in the out house. The teacher went out to see what they were doing and caught them playing doctor. She marched them back to the class room and each girl, one at a time, had to tell her what they had been doing. The punishment for each of the girls was they could only go to the out house one at a time. The teacher chaperoned them at recess by staying outside with them and making sure they followed her orders.

One day Mary Jo was going through peoples' lunches at recess. She was looking for cookies or candy and found some gum. She went outside to the play ground and was taking the gum out of the wrapper and Cousin Carol came walking over and asked, "Where did you get that gum? I bet you stole it." Mary Jo answered her, "I took it out of somebody's lunch sack." Carol said, "You should not be doing that." She did not tell the teacher or me because I never knew about it until this writing. We grew up never telling each other anything we did. Even when Mary Jo got caught she and our cousin kept it a secret between them.

Mary Jo and I have good memories of going to school at Berry Flat, when she stayed out of trouble. At recess the whole school would play the game of Annie Over. There were only about twenty children in the whole school first through the eight grades. There would be two teams, and two of the older students were the captains. They picked the teams from the rest of the students. The school had a pointed roof. They would call, "Annie" and the opposing side would call, "Over" and the ball would be thrown over the roof by the starting side. The opposing side would catch the ball and run around to the other side tagging everyone he could. Whoever was tagged would go with the person carrying the ball to their side. The object of the game was to not let anyone tag you, as you run around the building to the opposite side. That way your team stayed together. The winner ended up tagging everyone and bringing them over to their side. You could lose the ball if you dropped it and an opponent got hold of it. I would get my long legs running and I could run like a deer. Someone was always trying to outrun me and tag me.

The girls would play jump rope, hopscotch, and London Bridge was falling down. The boys would play marbles, softball, and basketball. The girls played marbles with the boys, I know I did. I remember the cat eye, steal marbles, and the large colored marbles. We always had something to play as a group. One day the third and fourth grades were playing under the trees in front of the school. A boy pulled some bark off the tree and was chewing it. The rest of us did the same thing and spit the juice out of our mouths like we were chewing tobacco. We even had it in our mouth going home on the bus and were spiting the juice in the bus. The bus driver put a stop to that real fast. He had to take a water hose to clean out the bus. Another time on the bus we were shooting spit wads in a rubber band sling shot. A boy was hit in the eye and that put a stop to that game.

We had to take care of the animals after school and on the week ends. Ray fed the pigs, he would mix corn and maze with water and let it sour. The pigs loved the sour mash along with the slop Mom saved from the vegetable peals and scrapes from the table. Richard milked the cows, and fed them cotton seed meal, corn, and maze. I had to feed the chickens maze, which was a grain, and gather the eggs.

About a week later, cousin John couldn't find his glasses. A few days later we went over to see Grandma and Grandpa and cousins John and Carol lived with them. Aunt Lois, Mom's old maid sister, lived with them and took care of John and Carol. Mary Jo was standing alone and Carol approached her and accused her, "You stole John's glasses." Mary Jo told her, "I did not steal John's glasses," and Carol did not believe her.

Mary Jo learned a valuable lesson that day. She did not want to be accused of taking something that she had not taken. She realized that once you are caught taking something that was not yours, you are labeled as a thief and you will be accused of taking something any time something goes missing. Mary Jo was cured of stealing that day. She never stole anything else.

Mom sold the eggs I gathered all week at Mansels' Grocery Store. She would put dresses on lay away for herself and us girls and make payments with the egg money. Easter was coming up and we were supposed to get a new dress for Easter. There was only one dress shop in O'Donnell. Mom went to the dress shop to make her weekly lay away payment and the proprietor told her she would have to pay for the dresses in full that day. She was closing up and moving to another town. Mom didn't have enough money to pay for the dresses. She went and told Dad and he gave her what cash he had, which was not enough. Mom went back to the dress shop and paid for her dress, Mary Jo and Annie's dresses and left me out. It broke my heart and I cried all the way home. I was so hurt that she put herself before me. She had a closet full of pretty dresses. We were lucky to get one new dress a year. She did finally buy me a new dress after Easter, but she had to wait until she went to another town.

One day I was driving Mom crazy saying, mama this, mama that, and mama, mama. I was asking her a lot of questions and she didn't want to answer. She was just sitting in a chair resting. Instead of telling me to shut up and go play she told me, "Don't call me mama." That got my attention. I felt crushed and my feelings were hurt. I ask her, "What I am suppose to call you." She did not answer me. I left her alone for a few days then just forgot it. I have not thought about it since she said it until now, at this writing. She never said anything like that to me again. I knew I would not ever say something like that to my children.

The school had a track meet and had to go to Gail, Texas to compete with other small schools. Richard won three first place ribbons and Ray thought he should have one. They got home around two o'clock in the afternoon. Ray was in the sixth grade and Richard was in the seventh grade. He was mad all the way home on the bus. When he got home he kept saying something about it and

popping off to Richard. Dad had enough and told him to shut up. Dad even shook him and he kept on complaining and fighting with Dad. He smarted off to Dad and ran and got a pitch fork. Dad got the pitch fork away from him and took his racier strap and whipped Ray. That all happened while I was at school and Mary Jo related the story to me when I got home. I noticed Ray had been crying and he would not talk about it. Richard told me the story years later. He wished he had given Ray one of his ribbons, if having a ribbon meant that much to him.

The day of the Halloween Party at school all the children could bring their mask to school. My sisters and I never had a mask to take to school. I know I always felt left out, like we were on the outside looking in and they felt the same way too. Mom would not buy us a mask, it could not have cost more than ten cents each. If we asked Dad for money he would give us a few pennies each.

We had to take an achievement test every year. I was in the third grade and three of us got a 100% correct on the test. That was the one and only time that ever happened to me. The teacher was so proud of us that she told us immediately. I never knew how I scored before, I guess the teacher didn't have to tell you unless you asked her.

When we moved from New Moore we took our dog Buster with us to the old home place. It must have been a couple of years later. One day I missed Buster when I was going to feed him, since that was my job. I called and called him. I ask every family member if they had seen him, and nobody acted like they even knew where he was. They claimed he must have ran away. I knew better than that. It was a couple days later, I was walking down the road, east of the house, and across the road where Uncle Bud, Mom's twin brother used to live. I found Buster. He had been ran over by a vehicle. Buster would not have been down on the road by himself, it was over a half mile from the house. I never did find out, who was with him when he got ran over or how it happened. It broke my heart, every time we lost an animal to death, to me it was like losing my best friend. I would go off by myself and cry.

That year the school had Christmas plays for the little kids and the big kids. The little kids play was about the Night before Christmas. The big room had a play of Jesus being born in a manger. They used some of the small children for angels. The partition between the grades first through fourth and fifth grades though eight grades was opened and pushed back into one large room. There was a stage in the big room. The night of the plays was a big event all the parents came to see the plays. Santa Clause arrived and passed out bags of fruit and candy. We had drawn names so the gifts were passed out also.

A lady from church called Sister Annie worked at the cafe in O'Donnell. One day Mom, my sisters and I stopped in to see her at work. While we were there Mom bought us three girls, hamburgers which cost fifteen cents each. It was the first and only time we ever got to eat hamburgers which were not made at home. Sister Annie was telling us about her tumble weed Christmas tree. We wanted to see it. The next time we came to town we stopped to see her and her tumble weed Christmas tree. A large tumble weed was setting on a table. It was decorated with lights, had fake snow sprayed on the branches, icicles, decorative ornaments, and strung popcorn like garland. It was pretty. Mary Jo and Annie wanted a tumble weed Christmas tree. The boys cut us a pine Christmas tree which we decorated. Dad ask the boys if they would rather have fruit, nuts, and candy for Christmas instead of a gift. They chose the fruit, nuts, and candy. Santa Clause came to see us girls and brought us dolls.

JW Zedlitz age 6
Richard Zedlitz age 1

Richard and Ray Zedlitz ages 11 and 10

Richard Zedlitz
Senior picture age 18, 1955

CHAPTER 8

The Year was 1951. Dad, Richard and Ray chopped cotton for other farmers. JW was drafted into the army during the Korean War. Each of us children wrote and sent him letters by air-mail for 6 cents. Regular postage at that time was 3 cents.

It was the first year Mom raised baby chickens and Dad bought 50 of the chicks. Dad made a pen in the chicken house to house the chicks. They didn't have mother hens to keep them warm. Dad took a light with a long extension cord, placed a 100 watt bulb in it, and lowered it within a couple feet above the chicks head. The light bulb kept the chicks warm. My job was to feed them twice a day. I would call them, "Biddy, biddy," and they would come running to meet me. I fed them grain and sometimes Mom would boil eggs and mash them, which I would feed to the chicks. They really loved the boiled eggs.

When the chicks were half grown and frying size. I was still feeding them. They would come running to be fed when ever I called them, "Biddy, biddy." Mom made me catch them one at a time and she would ring their necks to kill them. She scaled them in hot boiling water and Mary Jo and I would have to pluck all their feathers out. I had made pets out of the chickens and I could not eat chicken again. After the killing of the chickens, I would go off by myself and cry, then I would walk a mile to Grandma McDaniel's house and spend the day. When I got home I would bury the chicken bones in my pet cemetery. I had buried puppies, kittens, and even a gold fish that had died.

Mr. Blocker owned a grocery store in O'Donnell. He was the father of Dan Blocker, who played as Hoss Cartwright in Bonanza. Dan was in the Korean War the same time as JW was.

Mom and Dad would check with Mr. Blocker every week to see if he had heard from Dan. He sent Dan care packages. Dad paid Mr. Blocker to send JW care packages of goodies, the boxing, and mailing. JW would write and let us know when he got one. He told us of the soldiers who wouldn't get anything, and he would share his care pack with them. It was a surprise to hear he shared his care package with the soldiers. It was a thoughtful thing to do. He sure did not ever share any goodies with us.

Because of the drought and sand storms, Dad would have to borrow money from the Farmers Co-op to plant cotton and have money to buy food for a year. He told the proprietor of the R and W Grocery Store that he spent a $1000.00 a year on groceries. That is why he got mad when the Mansel Brothers' would put candy in the groceries for Dad to pay for. He thought they would charge him for someone's else bill, since he bought the groceries on credit. Dad had to work at the gin in the fall and winter until the cotton was all bailed. The money he made would help pay off the money he borrowed at the Farmers Co-op and the groceries he bought on credit.

Annie started to school that September. She would not talk to the teacher. The teacher told Mary Jo, a second grader, that if Annie didn't talk she would have to send her home. Mary Jo told Annie and she started to talking.

In the fall we would pick our own cotton after school and on week ends. We might only get a bail or two and our cotton would be picked. The farmers that had an irrigation system would still be picking cotton. Mom, Richard, Ray, Mary Jo, Annie and I would pick the cotton for a Mr. Ledbetter. Each of us girls would pick cotton in a gunny sack. We were too little to pull a six to eight foot cotton sack full. The most cotton I could pick to fill up the gunny sack or toe sack was 20 pounds and it was heavy for me to pull up to the scales to weigh the cotton. I sure could not throw the full sack over my shoulder and carry it. The money we made usually went for clothes. I did get to buy a leather purse with my initials HJZ burned on the side. I had to pay $3.00 for it and Mrs. Ledbetter made the purse for me. Mom paid her to make her one also.

The boys still had the bicycle. They planned to trade it for a 22 rifle. Before they did Mary Jo and I were trying to learn to ride the bicycle. It was a boy's bike and we were not tall enough to sit on the seat and reach the pedals. I had been trying but could not get the hang of it. Mary Jo was shorter than I and she was trying to do every thing I did. It was her turn to ride the bicycle. I held the bicycle while she got on the bike. I gave her a push and it started rolling. She headed straight to a barbed wire fence which was connected to the clothes line. She fell right on top of the bobbed wire fence and cut her leg. She needed stitches but she was not taken to a doctor and it did leave a scar.

A family from church gave us a German Shepherd when they were moving. We did not have him very long when he started sucking eggs. That was a no no because Mom sold eggs. I know she told Dad to get rid of him. He went missing and nobody knew what happened to him so he must of ran away. That was always the same old story when my dog disappeared. I knew better even at a very young age, if you feed an animal they did not run away. He ran to meet me every day because I fed him.

One day I was walking to the Berry Flat School, we must have missed the bus. I cannot think of any other reason to be walking to school. I was walking with Mary Jo and we took the short cut through the pasture. Low and behold we found the German Shepherd shot in the head. He had been dead for months. I knew Dad had shot him and I knew Mom had told him to. All Mom said when I jumped her when I got home after school was we cannot have a egg sucking dog on the farm.

At Christmas that year Mom and Dad bought a box of apples and a box of oranges. They bought a pound of mixed nuts, which you had to shell yourself, and one pound of hard ribbon candy. My sisters and I still believed in Santa Clause. Our Christmas tree that year had one string of lights, a box of icicles, garland, and a few decorative ornaments in different colors. We were so proud of that tree and we thought it was just beautiful.

That year Santa Clause brought me a doll and a tin set of pots and pans. Mary Jo and Annie got a doll and a red rocking chair each. They would sit in their rocking chairs in front of the heater to keep warm. We all would sit in front of the heater to keep warm. The boys chose to get the fruit and nuts instead of a gift for Christmas. Mom baked cakes and pies enough to last until New Years day. We all enjoyed every pie and cake Mom made.

Mom, Helen, Annie and Mary Jo Zedlitz, 1954

Richard Zedlitz age 16, 1952

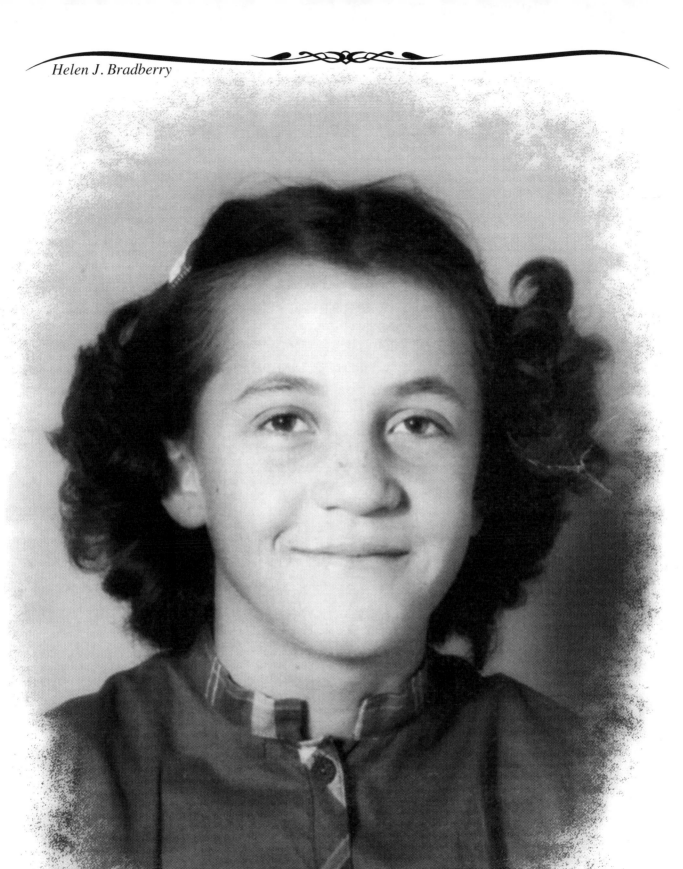

Helen Zedlitz age 11, 1953

CHAPTER 9

The New Year was 1952. That year Mom had surgery for cancer again. She was in the hospital for two weeks. My sisters and I stayed with Grandma and Grandpa McDaniel, Aunt Lois, and Uncle Lloyd until Mom came home from the hospital. Grandma and Aunt Lois would tell us stories and teach us songs that Grandma sang as a small child.

The accusations of corruption and Communism, the Truman-MacArthur dispute, and the continuing war in Korea became major issues of the 1952 election. President Harry S. Truman, who had served almost two full terms, decline to be a candidate again but helped secure the Democratic nomination for Governor Adlai E. Stevenson of Illinois.

On Valentine's Day, amazingly, we got valentines to exchange at school. We would give each person in the class a valentine and we would receive a valentine back from most of the children in the classes. The teacher gave each child candy hearts and a card.

There was a Mexican family who were as poor as we were. They didn't have any cards to give. I knew how they felt and always made sure I gave each of them a card. Even if I had to save the pennies Dad gave us to get the valentine cards. Two boys were in the same grade as I was and a girl was a grade ahead.

We would have to bring our colored eggs to school the Friday before Easter Sunday. Some children brought the colored candy eggs. The teacher would have a couple of the older children in the big room hide the eggs. The last couple of hours of the day we would have an Easter egg hunt. There was a pasture across the road in front of the school where they hid the eggs.

We never had an Easter Basket. My sisters and I would have to gather the eggs in our lunch

lord bucket or a sack. We gathered both candy eggs and colored eggs. The person who found the most eggs would win the prize, which was a chocolate rabbit.

Very few children would have an Easter Basket. We were all poor and didn't have the luxury of having one. There were always a few who had everything.

That summer at Berry Flat the girls in the 4 H Club would meet at someone's house. We baked cookies, cake, or made candy. We would eat what we made afterwards. The lady of the house would make us punch or cool-aid to drink. A lady picked us up and took us to the meeting and brought us home afterward. During the rest of the year, we had to make something for the County Fair at Gail, Texas. I hemmed a white, flour-sack dish-towel and received a third place ribbon.

Another time I was supposed to make an apron.   Mom did not sew, so I had to find someone willing to show me how to make one.   Lucy Fuller, a class mate of Richard, offered to help me. She showed me how to cut out the apron from a printed flower sack. I cut the apron out and she had to sew it on a treadle sewing machine. It was not run by electricity, you had to treadle with your feet back and forth to get it to sew.   I could not get the hang of it.   I did get a third place ribbon for the apron. The ribbons I received were always white.

One day the teacher checked a Mexican girl's hair and found lice in her hair.   Everyone in the first through the fourth grades got lice from the girl. My sisters and I had long hair and Aunt Lois cut our hair short. We had a special comb to comb the lice and eggs out of our hair. Mom got some medicine at the drug store to comb through our hair that was supposed to kill the lice. It must have worked on Mary Jo and Annie, they didn't have go through the kerosene treatment.

Aunt Lois came over to the house one Sunday afternoon and she with Moms help gave me the kerosene treatment. They washed my hair in water that had a spoonful of kerosene in it. It killed the lice and blistered my scalp. They had to rinse my hair a dozen time to get the smell out. My scalp was sore for a week. When anyone combed my hair, it felt like they were pulling out my hair by the roots. I have been tender headed ever since.

The boys collected funny books, better known as comic books. Richard even had a subscription to Donald Duck Comic Books. They bought the comic books at a used book store for a nickel each.   They would read the comic books which they bought each week, even if they had to sit up after bedtime. Once they read them, they did not read them again, so the comic books stacked up. They must have had a hundred of the comic books. They were stacked in a trunk to keep them out of Mom's way. They let me read them and when I got through with them, Mary Jo read the ones that she liked. She and I would have to go off to a place to read them after our chores were done. If we could have kept them they would have been collector items. No one remembers what happened to the comic books.

I suspect that they went the way as the Sears Roebuck catalog did, to the out door toilet to be used as toilet paper, after we cut out our paper dolls. Mom did not throw away anything that was paper, like brown paper bags etc. It went to the toilet to be used as toilet paper. Richard ask me, "Do you remember Mom ever buying toilet paper." I told him, "Yes, I did remember her buying toilet every week, she used it for her own needs." One of the things she did was buy Ponds face cream and used the toilet paper to wipe the cream off her face.

These stories were told to us by grandma, and some of the songs that she sang as a child, which she taught us, and we still remembered.

Helen Zedlitz age 14, 1956

*Cousin Carol, Helen, Cousin John,
Annie and Mary Jo, 1949*

Mary Jo Zedlitz age 10, 1954

CHAPTER 10

THE NEGRO AND THE MAN WITH RHEUMATISM

A Negro and a man crippled with rheumatism were walking down the road as it was getting dark. They walked by a cemetery. When they reached the gate, they heard voices coming from inside the cemetery. They heard, "One for you and one for me, one for you and one for me, one for you and I will get that one at the gate." When they heard, "I will get that one at the gate," it scared the man crippled with rheumatism so bad that he out ran the Negro getting home.

Two boys were in the cemetery counting out their peanuts. The boy carrying the bag of peanuts dropped one of the peanuts at the gate. The Negro and the man with rheumatism thought it was God and the devil counting out lost souls in the cemetery and a lost soul was standing at the gate. They did not intend to be one of the lost souls standing at the gate.

THE BANANA

The first time Grandma McDaniel ate a banana was when she was a small child back in the 1890's. A friend of the family gave her a banana, she looked at it wondering how to eat it. She pulled the peel back and saw the core. So she threw the core away and ate the peel. She did not like it. The next time she saw the family's friend, he ask her, "How did you like the banana?" and she told him, she didn't like it and why. He then told her, "You threw the banana away and ate the peel." What she thought was the core was the banana. The next time she got a banana she ate it the right way and liked it.

THE UNFRIENDLY LADY

Grandma McDaniel rarely ever got to go to town. They would have to go in a wagon being pulled by a horse. If the town was over a day's ride, they would have to camp out over night before they got there and do the same thing going back home. This time she did get to go to town. She had never seen herself in a mirror and did not know what she looked like. She was about twelve years old. She was walking down the board walk and saw her reflection in the window. She said, "Hello" and no one answered, so she said, "Hello" again, still no answer. She told her mother about it. Her mother said, "that was your reflection that you saw in the window and of course you would not get a response."

THE PEANUT

I found a peanut, a peanut, a peanut;
I found a peanut, just now.
Where did you find it at, find it at, find it at;
Where did you find it at just now?
I found it in the wood box, the wood box, the wood box;
I found it in the wood box just now.
What did it taste like, taste like, taste like;
What did it taste like, just now?
It tasted like a peanut, a peanut, a peanut;
It tasted like a peanut just now.

THE OLD BLUE JAY

I caught an old blue jay by the tail, by the tail, by the tail, E I O.
I took him to the house and picked him clean, picked him clean, picked him clean, E I O.
I put him in a skillet and fried him brown, fried him brown, fried him brown, E I O.
I took a little jump and swallowed him down, swallowed him down, swallowed him down,
E I O.
That was the last of the old blue jay, the old blue jay, the old blue jay, E I O.

OH WHERE IS MY KITTY

Oh, where is my kitty, my little gray kitty, I looked the house all around.
I looked in the cradle, and under the table, but no where could kitty be found.
I took my dog, Rover, and looked the fields over, no dog could be kinder, but he

could not find her, so I had to give up in despair.
Oh, where is my kitty, my little gray kitty, I looked the house all around.
I looked in the cradle, and under the table, but no where could kitty be found.
I took my hook, and I went to the brook, to see if poor kitty was there.
But when I had found her, the old brook had drowned her, so I had to give up in despair.
I took my spade, and I went to the shade, to dig poor kitty a grave.
I lay her away on a bright sunny day, so the leaves could blow over her grave.

These songs and one of the stories are over 100 years old. My Grandma McDaniel read and sang them when she was a child.

Mary Jo, Annie, and I sang this song, "Oh Where is my Kitty," on stage at Berry Flat when we were given a day to entertain the other children. Some of the students would sing and play the guitar, recite a poem, or tell a story. We were in the first, second, and third grades.

Family Photo: 1950
Mom, Richard, Ray, Dad,
Mary Jo, Helen and Annie

Group picture Richard and Ray with cousins
Aaron and James Zedlitz at house on farm in
Borden County, Texas. Mom and Helen
& cousins Florence and Janice Zedlitz
in door way.

Annie Zedlitz age 15, 1960

CHAPTER 11

JW wrote and told us, he was coming home on leave on a certain day. We went to pick him up at the bus station in O'Donnell. He did not show up. We received a letter a couple of weeks later with some pictures of a ship, he was on his way to Korea. Of course, Mom started crying. Dad requested prayer at church for JW, weekly, for the next two years. During that year he sent us pictures of himself, some of the guys in his squadron, the fox holes that they had to fight out of, and a bar in Japan with pretty Geisha girls.

PAPER DOLLS AND MUD HOUSES

My sisters and I had a lot of fun playing with paper dolls. We would play for hours that summer of 1952. We cut out our paper dolls from a Sears Roebuck catalog. I was the oldest, so I always made the first choice. We would cut out a pretty lady, a father, children, clothes, and furniture. We would cut out a picture of a house and a car and pretend the house and car were ours. We played on the floor setting up the house with rooms of fine furniture, pretending that there was a closet for the clothes. We used a box or lid to a shoe box and placed the picture of the car on it to push our paper dolls around. We each had our own paper doll house layout on the floor. We would put our paper doll family in our fine car, go visit each other, go to church, and go through the motions of acting out the singing and preaching to our paper dolls. When we were through playing, we would have to pick them up and put them away to play another day. Mom would all ways threaten us that if she had to pick them up, she would put them in the trash, and she would have, so we took her at her word. That included anything we would be playing with, and even our clothes. All of us children had to pick up after ourselves.

On warm sunny days and when the sand storms weren't blowing, we would play out side and make mud houses. We used hair oil bottles, which were flat on two sides, as our cars. I took a spade and made roads between our mud houses. The bottles could slide on the ground as we pushed them. We used small sticks for our mom, dad, and children. One time I used a small nail as the baby.

One day we took our stick family to the lake, a pond that the cows drank out of, which was ground level. We would put the sticks in the water to swim. The sticks would float on top of the water. I put the baby nail in the water and it sank to the bottom. I had forgotten that nails did not float. My stick family's baby drowned. I was crying and carrying on as if someone had really died. Annie, finally tired of my carrying on, told me, "You need to find another nail to use for your baby." I didn't want another nail. I needed to have a funeral for that baby.

When the cow had a calf, Dad would keep the first bull to kill for meat. If a heifer was born. The oldest son would get the heifer. If the heifer had a calf, JW could sell it or keep it. If Dad's cow had another bull and we did not need it for meat, it went to the second son, who was Richard then Ray. While Richard was gone, chopping cotton for a farmer, his steer got out of his pen. He got into some freshly cut corn stocks or maize and ate too much. The steer blotted up with gases and needed some help.

Dad went over to another farmer's house to get some advice. He came back with a soda bottle filled with baking soda and water mixed. He feed it to the steer but it did not help. The steer was getting sicker. He was lying down next to the water, but could not get to the water. Dad took a sharp knife and stabbed the steer between the rib cage and the hind leg. He was trying to release some of the gases from the stomach. It was late in the afternoon, the sun was going down, and the steer died right before our eyes. There was not a Veterinary Clinic in O'Donnell. When Richard came home, he found out about the steer dieing. I told him the story of how it died. The next day Dad removed the hide from the carcass and threw the carcass out in the field for the vultures to get too.

We had to carry the water to the house from the windmill for us to drink, Mom to cook with, and all of us to take a bath in. The windmill was two hundred feet from the house. The bucket was too big for me to carry full. I splashed out half the water on my feet before I would get to the house. Mom would heat the water in a tea kettle on the stove. We used a # 2 wash tub to bathe in. If the boys didn't bring the water into the house to pour in the tub, I would have to make a dozen trips back and forth to carry the water in from the windmill. It was bath day and Mary Jo was trying to be helpful. She pushed a chair up to the stove, climbed up on the chair, picked the boiling kettle of water up, and got down off the chair without spilling any water. She took the kettle of hot water over to the tub, poured the water into the tub. The lid was not put on right, however, the lid fell off and scalded her hand with boiling water. Mom didn't have anything to put on her hand. Mary Jo ran to the windmill and soaked her hand in the cold water being pumped out into the barrel.

Mom told me, "Helen, go to Grandma's house to get some vinegar and baking soda." She lived a mile from us. I ran as far as I could, walked until I could get my breath, and started running again until I got there. I told Grandma what happened. She gave me the vinegar and baking soda, and I ran and walked the same way going back home. When I got home Mom made up a wash pan

of vinegar, water, and baking soda for Mary Jo to soak her hand in. Her poor hand was covered with a water blister. The vinegar and soda did take the pain out of her burn. We finally did get to take a bath without any more problems.

I loved to drink coffee as a child. Mom and Grandma fed us coffee as babies. The coffee was mostly milk. I would use milk in my coffee as long as the cow gave milk. If the cow was with calf, the cow dried up. When the calf was born it nursed two of the mother cow's tits. Richard milked the cow's other two tits until the calf was weaned. The calf would be separated from the cow or the calf would nurse all the cow's milk and we would not have any milk. I learned to drink coffee without milk. Mom thought I used too much sugar in my coffee, so she took that away from me too. I learned to drink the coffee black without milk or sugar.

After Richard milked the cow, Mom would let the milk set in the refrigerator until it cooled down and the cream would rise to the top. She skimmed the cream off the milk, put it into a fruit jar, and let it sour. Mary Jo and I had to churn the cream in the jar by shaking it up and down until the kernels of butter formed. We then poured the excess sour milk off the kernels, added salt, and mashed the kernels and salt together and put it into a bowl. We had real butter for our hot biscuits for breakfast.

It was Christmas of 1952. Times are hard and we are very poor. The drought was still going on and we had not had a decent cotton crop in two years. We only gathered two bails of cotton that year. I was 10 years old when I received the shock of my life. The school bus had dropped us off and I was the first one to get to the house. There was a car parked in the drive way and I knew Mom had company. It was a couple of women who were neighbors in the community. They had children that we went to school with. As I opened the door to go into the house, I heard Mom talking and bad mouthing Dad. She said, "John was a crazy old fool and so was his whole family." I stood there in shock and the ladies looked up and saw me. They got up and left right away and never came back. I asked Mom, "Why did you say that to the ladies? You know that they have children that we go to school with and they will tell them what you said." We are already branded as poor, white, trash now we would be branded as crazy, poor, white, trash. We had Mom to thank for that. She didn't even care. Anytime I saw the women after that I felt ashamed of what Mom had done. I knew they would tell everybody in the community, because of the way they acted. If they happened to meet Mom or Dad on the street, they weren't very friendly and might not even speak at all. I know Dad picked it up right away. I could never tell him. He even commented about the unfriendly actions of the people he had known for years.

The only terms of endearment we ever heard from Mom, when she would speak of Dad, was that he was an old crazy fool. The only terms of endearment we ever heard from Dad when he would speak of Mom was that she was an old dirty hog. Of course they never said that to each other in person. Dad never said that to anyone else, only when he was talking to us children. We never heard the words I love you. We never received a hug from Mom or Dad. Hugs were only reserved for the baby and as she got older she didn't receive any hugs either.

We still picked what little cotton Dad grew and also picked cotton for a neighbor Mr. Ledbetter. Dad went to work at a cotton gin to make ends meet.

Santa Clause did come and brought my sisters and I ugly dolls for Christmas. Grandma, Uncle Lloyd, and Aunt Lois came over for Christmas dinner. When Aunt Lois saw our dolls she said, "Those dolls are so ugly they ought to be burned." We did not agree with her. We were happy to get anything to play with. We did play with the dolls until they went missing. I accused the boys of burning our dolls. They denied it of course. I know one of them did and will always believe it.

JW was suppose to come home on leave from Korea. We went to the bus station to meet him on the day he was supposed to be there. The last bus came in. JW was not there again. Mom and Dad were worried because we didn't know what could have happened. A day or two later we heard on the news that a plane had crashed bringing solders home from Korea. We were all afraid and Dad continued requesting prayer for JW's safety at church on Sundays. It must have been a couple of weeks later when we received a letter from JW. He was in a hospital in Japan for hemorrhoid surgery. I found out later he did not want Mom to know the truth.

Dad takes us to church every Sunday when he is able to. The church is in O'Donnell. He has to drive sixteen miles to get there. The Huston family was a neighbor, who lives about five miles from us. They go to the same church as we do. They were going to move to a small town near Lubbock. They need to go find a place to live. Mr. Houston asked Dad if Richard and Ray could take care of his cows and chickens until he got back to move them. Dad told him, "Yes, Richard and Ray could do that for you."

There was a peach tree in the back yard. Peaches were falling on the ground and hanging over ripe on the tree. Mom had us girls pick up the peaches lying on the ground that didn't have ants in them. She picked the overripe peaches from the tree. We took the peaches home. Mom made peach cobblers, pies, and jelly out of the peaches. They were so good. We had only eaten canned peaches from a store. They sure did not taste the same as a fresh cooked peach.

Richard drives us to Sunday school while dad is working at the cotton gin in another town. One Sunday a woman from the church approached Richard and accused him of stealing $40.00 of the church money from the Houston's' house. It appeared that Mrs. Houston was the church treasurer. Richard did not know what she was even talking about. He had never been near the house and told her so. The house had been locked up like Fort Knox. The only person that had been in the house had a key and he told her so. Mom had told all of us to stay away from the house. If something went missing we would be blamed. I knew something was wrong but nobody told me anything. For years I believed we were accused of stealing the overripe peaches. Fifty years pass when Richard finally told me the truth when I asked him. Richard and Mom found out later that one of the Houston's' boys had come home from the Navy and found the money and spent it. Richard never received an apology from anyone in the church. That was a good example of someone jumping to conclusions before they knew the facts. He never went back to that church again.

CHAPTER 12

Grandpa, Grandma McDaniel, Uncle Lloyd and Aunt Lois were getting ready to move to Lubbock, Texas. Grandpa had a cow that Mom's twin brother had given him years before. This cow had several calf's. Grandpa needed to sell them so they would have the money to move. Uncle Bud threw a fit and wanted the money that would come out of the sell of the cattle. He figured since he gave them the cow, he was entitled to the money. Dad came to Grandpa's rescue and bought the cow and gave the money to Grandpa. I don't know who bought the calf's but they were sold too and the money went to Grandpa. Grandpa never spoke to Uncle Bud again. Uncle Bud never spoke to Dad again. The next time we saw him was at Grandpa's funeral.

Grandma, Grandpa, Uncle Lloyd, and Aunt Lois moved to Lubbock, Texas, in 1953. Aunt Lois wanted me to come to Lubbock that summer and do their laundry. She knew I was doing the laundry at home for our family and had been doing it for a whole year. I turned 11 years old that March. Dad only let me stay a month.

My cousins, Carol and John were living with their mother, Aunt Maudie, her husband and two little kids. Carol and I were the same age. Carol stayed with me at Grandma's. When her stepfather came over to pick her up, she would want me to go home with her. I could go as long as I came back to the laundry one day each week. Her stepfather took us all to the baseball game and bought us hot dogs and pop corn. I had never been to a professional ball game before. I went to two of the games while I was there. He took me back to Grandma's after a day or two. While I was at Carol's house, we did the dishes, mopped floors, and ironed clothes. I didn't go over there

and sit down and have my aunt wait on me.

I went back to Grandma's house and once a week I spent the day doing the laundry. The washer machine was a ringer washing machine. I had to put hot water in the washer to wash the clothes. There was a hot water heater in the house, so I did not have to boil water on the stove. I filled the three rinse tubs with cold water using a bucket. The tubs were #2 wash tubs, which are round and very large. I used the same water to wash and rinse all the clothes in. Aunt Lois would sort the clothes in a pile of whites, sheets towels and washcloths and maybe two piles of colored clothes. Grandpa's overalls were washed separate from the other clothes because they might stain every thing blue. I would wash and run the clothes through the ringer into each tub of rinse water, then into a basket to hang out the clothes on the clothes' line in the back yard.

After all the clothes were hung on the line to dry, I emptied the washer and tubs with the same bucket, I filled them with. I mopped the floor because I always managed to spill some of the water on my feet. Once the clothes were dry, I would take them of the clothes' line, bring them in, fold them up, and put them away. I did this once a week for four weeks and Aunt Lois gave me $ 1.50. I would call that slave labor in todays standards.

Grandma and I would sit on the porch in the late afternoons and at night until bed time. She would tell me stories of her life when she was a young girl. She told me about dating Grandpa. They couldn't hold hands until they were engaged to be married. I ask her, "How did you know you loved each other if you could not even hold hands, let a lone kiss each other?"

She told me, "You will know when you love somebody by just being with them and when you grow up you will know." That was hard to believe when I was only 11 years old.

Carol and her stepfather came over. I went home with them. When we got to their house Aunt Maudie was mad. My cousin John told me, "She does not want you here." If I had a way I would have left right then and gone back to Grandma's. I was so hurt and I had to wait until my Uncle would take me back to Grandma's. He got in trouble for taking me to their home. While I was there I still washed dishes, mopped floors, and ironed clothes. When I finally got to go back to Grandma's, Carol stayed a day or two. When her stepfather came to pick her up, she ask if I could go to, and he said, "No."

I told her I would not go back over there. I don't know why she even ask him. Aunt Maudie acted mad at Aunt Lois. She did not know why, and I could not tell her because Aunt Maudie did not want me over there. I never spent another minute at her house unless Mom was with us. She tried to get us girls to stay with her one time while Mom was visiting Grandma. Mary Jo and Annie did but I would not stay. That was the last time I ever saw her and her family. I heard that she had 9 more kids. If she didn't like kids, God sure blessed her with lot of them. I never told anyone about how Aunt Maudie acted.

The only difference in doing laundry for Aunt Lois and doing it at home was that, Mom would have the boys bring in the water to the house from the windmill. They would fill up the tubs with rinse water. Mom would heat the wash water on the stove. I would have to climb upon a chair to dip the water out of the tub to put into the washer. I washed each tub full of clothes and rinsed them twice.

I would have to hang clothes out on the clothes' line, when I was too short to reach the line. Mom would have to hang out the sheets first, the weight of the sheets would lower the clothes line, where I could reach it. After all the clothes were hung out, I would empty the washer and both tubs of water. I had to use a bucket to drain the water out of the wash machine and empty the water outside. I had to dip the water out of the tubs with a bucket and dump the water outside on the ground. When the clothes were dry, Mary Jo and I would bring them in, fold them up, and put them away. I never told Mom about ironing clothes for Aunt Maudie or she would have had me ironing clothes too.

Dad had a radio that Mom played all-day, listening to country music. It was run by electricity or a battery big enough to put in a car. It ran on a 9 volt or 12 volt battery. Dad would listen to gospel music out of Del Rio, Texas until he went to bed at night. Richard ordered a harmonica, that you could make say mama, from the radio advertisement for a dollar. When he received it, what a disappointment, it was red plastic harmonica which cost about ten cents in a five and ten cent store. He never learned how to make the harmonica say mama.

Berry Flat was closing down. It has been consolidated with another small school. A new school was being built. It would be called Plains School. Grades first through the sixth grade went to this school. The school was still a mile from the house in the opposite direction. We still had to ride a bus. The older kids had to ride a bus to Gail, Texas, a new school was being built, grades first through twelfth grade. The boys had to ride the bus about 20 miles to school one way.

One of Eisenhower's campaign pledges had been to end the Korean Conflict, and a truce was achieved in 1953.

JW wrote us again the war was over and he was coming home on the bus again. His tour of duty was over and he was coming home for good. We went to meet him at the bus station again. He did not show up. He did come in a couple of days later and he had to catch a ride out to the house. He got a job making terraces for other farmers around Texas and Kansas. We did not see to much of him.

We started to the new school called Plains, in September. I was the only girl in the fourth grade. Mary Jo was in the third grade and Annie was in the second grade. We did not have any friends to play with so Mary Jo and I played together.

Dad bought the piano from the Berry Flat School before the school was torn down. It was an upright, weighed a ton, and it took four or five people to move it. Mary Jo and I took piano lessons from the new music teacher at Plains School. We even competed in a recital in Gail, Texas that year.

Each class has a princess chosen by the class. Since I was the only girl in my class, I became the princess of the fourth grade. I was the tallest person in school. I was even taller than the boys. Each princess picked a prince out of the class. I chose a boy who was almost as tall as I. We collected money any where we could. The princess who collected the most money would be crowned Queen. We all wore formal dresses to the crowning on Halloween night. Mom was able to buy a dress from one of the neighbors who had an older girl, who had out grown the formal dress. Mom paid $5.00 for the red formal dress. Red was my favorite color. All the families were

coming to the party. A girl, Dee Dee Burrer, in the fifth grade was crowned queen of the ball. The Halloween carnival was on the same night and the first one my sisters and I had ever been to.

The boys were playing at a basketball game one night at another school. They were already at the school when the sand storm hit. It blew all night and the boys had to spend the night in the gym at school. The bus driver could not bring the boys home. They did not make it home until the next afternoon. Mom and Dad were worried about them. I could feel the fear and stress and I was afraid for the first time in my life about somebody other than myself.

My sisters and I wore hand-me-down clothes, these clothes given to us from older siblings of girls we went to school with. Whenever the girls would see us with a dress on their sisters had worn, they would say, "That was my sister's dress." I would answer back, "Yes, it's a very nice dress and I am glad to have it." They would usually leave me alone. Dad planted cotton that year but there was not enough rain for the cotton to come up. That year was a very poor year. We did not have one bail of cotton to pick that year.

JW was still working making terraces for farmers. He wanted Dad to move back to New Mexico, where there were no sand storms. The farm needed an irrigation system and it was going to cost too much for Dad to put one in on the old home place.

At school we practiced for a play. I had a small part in the play. The play was set for the last day before Christmas break, which was going to last two weeks. The night of the play Richard was not there and Dad was still working at the gin in another town. Ray was going to drive me to the play. The car would not start. He and I had to push the car. We could not push the car fast enough for him to pop the clutch and start the car. I didn't get to go to the play. Mr. Baker was my teacher and he was madder than a hornet. Richard was at the school waiting for us to get there, when we did not show up he ran all the way home. Mr. Baker came out the next day to see why I had not showed up. Mom told him why and he had to be satisfied with the reason. We did not have a phone, so there was no way to get a hold of anyone. No one was concerned enough the night before to come out to check to see if there was a problem. I had never missed any function that I had to be in before.

While Dad was working at the gin, he had a stroke. His face was twisted and he had trouble using his right arm and hand. He had to come home and go to the doctor. The boys drove Mom and us girls to pick up Dad in another town and bring him home. Dad was unable to work.

It was going to be a very poor Christmas that year. We went through the motions of putting up a tree that the boys cut. We used the same lights, a few icicles, and a few decorative ornaments, from the previous Christmas to hang on the tree. We had made a few ornaments at school and we used them also. We still thought the tree was pretty.

The Sheriff of Borden County surprised us one day before Christmas. He brought us boxes of food and each of us girls a doll. The dolls were the nicest we had ever had. I don't recall the boys getting anything. We did have a nice Christmas dinner. It turned out to be a good Christmas for us girls that year.

CHAPTER 13

In the 1950's, Art Linkletter had a TV show about the funny things that children say. He would ask a child a question and the answer would be hilarious. The show reminded me of a memory of an incident that was told to us girls when we were younger. Richard was a small child, maybe three or fours years old. He was with Dad in the meat market of the grocery store. Dad and the butcher were talking. The butcher looked down at Richard and asked him, "Would you eat an old, dead chicken," and he promptly answered, "No, I will not eat an old, dead chicken." Dad and the butcher had a good laugh at his answer. He was thinking of a dead chicken that he seen lying on the ground in the yard. He knew he sure wouldn't eat that chicken.

The New Year was 1954. JW was still trying to get Dad to sell the farm and move to New Mexico. There had been a drought the last three years. You cannot grown cotton unless you have an irrigation system. Dad had been unable to work but was recovering. One of the farmers who was a neighbor offered to buy the farm. He would pay him $15,000.00 for the 160 acres. Dad sold the farm and we moved to Roswell, New Mexico again. We want be moving back to Texas again. I think we were glad to be moving, I know I was. I never went back to see the old home place, some of the family members did.

Dad found a farm and a house to live in on Oldrof's farm. It was a very old two story house with a wrap around porch on front and one side of the house. It was built on high ground two hundred feet from the Berrendo River. There were three bedrooms up stairs, one was used as a bedroom, Mary Jo and Annie played house in one room, and the third room floor was falling in; you could not walk in there. Mom's bedroom was underneath that room on the ground floor.

There was some history to this house. It was said that Pat Garrett, the Sheriff of Lincoln County, had lived in this house in his later years. He was the one who killed Billy the Kid.

One Sunday, Dad and I had gone to church; we came home and had dinner. I was sitting in the living room reading. Mary Jo came prancing from the entry hall, through the living room where I was reading, heading toward the door to Mom's bedroom. We both heard a crack in the ceiling in Mom's bedroom. When I heard the crack I looked up to see what she doing. She looked up as she reached the door. She turned around and was moving so fast back to the entry hall, that she was in the entry hall when the ceiling hit the floor in Mom's bed room. I though I was going to die laughing at her. She was moving so fast, like a streak of lightning. I have had a lot of chuckles through the years when I thought of the incident.

One afternoon I was washing clothes on the ringer washing machine; there were two tubs for rinsing the clothes in. I was in the dinning room, running the clothes through the ringer into the rinse water. I was being careful because I did not want by hand to go through the ringer up to my arm. I had seen Mary Jo do it before and it would jam and somebody needed to be there to unplug the washer.

I was running the last load out into a basket which I would carry outside to hang the clothes on the cloth's line. Ray, Mom, Mary Jo, and Annie had gone to haul water in a water tank. They went over to Uncle Paul's farm which was a couple miles from the house. We could not drink the water on the farm. I believe the water was pumped out of the Berrendo River. Dad, JW, Richard and Uncle Dan, who was staying with us for a while, were working in the field. I knew I was alone in the house. The radio was on and I was singing along with it.

I heard a noise. It sounded like something heavy bouncing down the stairs one step at a time. It scared me so bad I forgot to take the clothes out to hang on the clothesline. I was getting out of there so fast I almost fell down the steps of the back porch. I stayed outside until Mom, Ray and the girls got home. I told Ray about something falling down the stairs. We both looked at the bottom of the stairs; there was nothing there. We went up stairs to see if anything had fallen up there, nothing was found. We found no explanation for the noise on the stairs. I know what I heard.

The stairs were very steep. Mary Jo and I each fell down the stairs once that year. I slipped and fell bouncing down each step on my bottom. Mary Jo slipped and fell bouncing down each step on her knees. After that we walked down the stairs a little more carefully.

It rained so much that year of 1954, that it flooded twice. The Berrendo River overflowed and the water came up to within a few feet of the front porch. Thank God the house was built on high ground. We had to miss school a couple of weeks until the water went down and the bridge across the Berrenda River was checked for damage. Any of the children who lived on our side of the river couldn't get to school because nobody could get across the river. I have been afraid of water ever since, and that was why I was never able to learn to swim.

A lot of people would come out to the Berrendo River to swim. We found a brown paper bag full of True Stories someone had left at the river. Mary Jo and I read everyone of the True Stories. That was my first time to see or hear of the word sex. Mom should not have let us read them.

One of the boys had a subscription for the Tarzan and Jane Comic Book. Mary Jo would go to the mail box and be the first one to read it. I usually would read it on a Sunday afternoon after church when we received it.

Ray, my sisters, and I went to Berrendo School that year. I was in the last half of the fifth grade. Ray was in the eight grade. Mary Jo was in the fourth grade and Annie was in the third grade. Mary Jo and I were in the same room. I had to take a test on the first half of a history book I had never had a lesson in before. The only part I had study was on World War II. I failed the semester test. I did good on the daily lessons. It was very hard changing schools in the middle of the year and coming from another state.

Ray had a hard time in the eight grade so he quit school. I passed to the sixth grade. Mary Jo failed the fourth grade and would be repeating it in September. Annie failed the third grade and had to repeat it also. Richard was a sophomore and passed. He was going into his junior year at high school in Roswell.

My three brothers and Uncle Dan would go to the drive-in picture show at night sometimes. It cost a buck a car load so you could fill up a car with as many people as could ride safely. JW also bought the first TV. It was black and white, 19 inch screen, and only one TV channel to watch, which was channel 8. We would all sit around the TV at night watching channel 8. The programs lasted 30 minutes each, and the TV was always turned off at 9 o'clock.

Dad and JW farmed cotton, soy beans, and alfalfa hay that year. Because of the two floods, Dad didn't have to do a lot of irrigating that year. He was still recovering from the stroke. Mr. Oldrof sold the farm and we had to move again.

*Friend Sue Morrison and Helen Zedlitz on
steps of North Junion School, 1958*

CHAPTER 14

Dad had to find another farm. He found a farm located 40 miles east of Roswell. The farmer had a heart attack and need someone to farm the land until he got well. The farm only had two small houses like a workers camp to live in. One house had a kitchen and a large room we used for the living room and bedroom. My sisters and I slept in the bed. Mom slept on a roll-away bed. The roll-away bed was folded up during the day and let out at night to sleep on.

The second house was next door and it was big enough to hold three double beds and a chest of drawers. Dad, JW, and the two boys slept out there.

We still went to Berrendo School. A small bus picked us up a mile from the farm. Richard or Ray drove us to the bus stop to catch the bus. We left the car there to ride home in. We left the house before sun up and came home after dark that year of 1955 during the fall and winter months.

I was twelve years old and in the sixth grade. My class was too large and six of us were moved into the seventh grade room. Ray went back to school and started in the ninth grade. Richard was a junior in high school. Mary Jo and Annie were repeating the third and fourth grades.

Mom had to go to the hospital and have surgery, she had a sore on her foot and it had to have tissue grafted in to the sore. She had scratched her foot with a nail in the screen door. We girls stayed with Aunt Ella while this was being done. She asked a question I had been wondering about for six years. I told her, " I remembered Mom and Aunt Lizzy having a screaming match after we first moved to the old home place and went up to see them." We left and went back home and Mom had been crying but I had never known why or what happened. She asked me if I remembered a black lunch bucket. I told her, "Yes I did and I remembered Mom making lunch

and putting it into the lunch bucket, for Cousin Fred, and the bucket set on the floor in the kitchen when it was not being used."

Aunt Lizzie wrote and told all of Dad's sisters that Mom let one of her nasty children, meaning Mary Jo, Annie, or me, use the lunch bucket to go to the bathroom in. We did use a slop jug or a bucket at night. We did not have a bathroom in the house. We were too afraid of the dark to go outside or even into another dark room in the middle of the night. Cousin Fred discovered what was in his lunch bucket at lunch when he opened it to eat his lunch. I could not believe Mom had let anyone use that lunch bucket like that. I was seven years old and I knew I sure didn't do it. Mary Jo and Annie didn't remember doing such a thing. Mom never admitted to anyone if she let Annie or Mary Jo do such a thing. Why didn't she find it, if she had made his lunch for the next day? The thought ran through my mind of what Dad called Mom. Only an old dirty hog would have let something like that happen.

We had a dog named Smokey and he was a small dog. We brought him with us from Texas. He was run over by running under the tire of a cotton trailer that JW was pulling with a tractor. He did not die right away. He lived three days, then died and one of the boys buried him on the farm.

The farm was near the Rio Grande River. The river was dry except in certain spots and a tinkle of water would flow around the sand barges. The owner of the farm lived on the other side of the river. He drove across the river to get to our side. There were thousands of acres of desert land around us.

Dad and JW carried a 30/30 rifle every time they drove to Roswell to get groceries. There were hundreds of jack rabbits and some rattled snakes. They shot them to keep them from eating the young and tender cotton plants. I hated to be with them when they shot the jack rabbits. The rabbits actually screamed and jumped into the air when they were shot. We never ate one of them because they were full of worms and could have had rabies. If they saw a rattled snake on the road they would stop and kill the snake.

We never had a chance to take piano lessons again, after we left Texas. I practiced and taught myself a lot. Yes, we moved the two ton piano everywhere we moved. I was even backup piano player at Salt Creek Baptist Church. Dad drove us twenty miles to the church, when we got to go.

I turned thirteen that March. A neighbor lady made me a chocolate cake with white frosting made with egg whites and white corn syrup. It was so good, and I was not expecting it when we came home from school. I was hoping that Mom had made me a cake.

Each year Dad signed up for Mexican Nationals through the Farmers Co-op working with immigration. He would be assigned ten to twelve workers to pick cotton. The farmers had to furnish them a place to live. There were usually a workers' camp to house the Mexicans. Dad went to the Salvation Army Store to buy the things the Mexicans would need the first time. He bought cots, army blankets, towels and wash clothes, pots, pans, and dishes for them to use. He had some of the things left over from the year before. He was careful with the things the mice would eat up. Mice would take over an empty house or storage shed if poison was not set out. There were kangaroo rats out in the desert land. They hopped on their hind legs like a kangaroo.

When the Mexicans arrived from Mexico, Dad was there to pick them up. He bought them

food for a week until they earned their first week's wage. He took the money for the advanced food out of the money they earned the first week they worked. Dad or JW drove them back and forth to the field and to town to get their groceries.

Dad never let the Mexican get close to us girls. We were still children, but I looked older than I was, probably because I was 5 foot 7 inches tall.

That first year there was a young Mexican 17 year's old working with his Dad. The young man saw me from a distance and I had never even spoke a word to him. If he had we couldn't have under stood each other. I did not speak Spanish and he did not speak English. He gave Ray or Richard a love letter to give to me and one of them did give me the letter just to aggravate me. Of course I could not read it, the letter was written in Spanish. I went to school with Mexican children, and I took it to school to see if anybody could read it. One girl, who rode the bus with us, recognized a few words and told me it was a love letter.

One of the Mexican workers had pneumonia and spent a week in the hospital. Dad paid the hospital bill. When he was released he walked out of the hospital and disappeared.

When the cotton had been picked, Dad returned the Mexicans to the Farmers Co-op working through immigration to be returned to Mexico. We never found out if the Mexican was ever caught and returned to Mexico.

We were still going to Berrendo School. I broke my little finger that year playing softball. I had to wear a cast for six week, and then soak it in warm water to get it to bend.

We had PE one day a week when every girl could wear jeans to play in. A coach would be there that one day a week. We played volleyball, basketball, or softball. My sisters and I never had any jeans to wear on that day.

Grandpa McDaniel died on December 20, 1955, of a heart attack and was buried on Christmas Eve. Richard and Ray drove Mom and us girls to Lubbock, Texas for the funeral. The Williams and the Stags came from O'Donnell to the funeral to be Casket Bearers. That was the first time Mom saw her twin brother, Uncle Bud, since the blow up over the cow and calves with Grandpa when they moved to Lubbock, Texas in 1953.

CHAPTER 15

Uncle Lloyd married and his wife, Aunt Jean, had two teenage children. I only saw the girl once. Aunt Jean asks me, what was I getting for Christmas I told her, "A billfold." She looked surprised. What I didn't tell her was that I was paying for it out of my money I made for picking cotton. Otherwise I would have told her that I was not getting anything. Then she would really looked surprised.

It was 1956, and we were moving again. The land owner recuperated from his heart attack. We were moving into two small houses again. One house had the kitchen and a living room and bedroom, two rooms in one house and one room in the second house. Dad and the boys slept in the one room house. It held three double beds and a chest of drawers.

It did have electricity but no water piped into the house. The water we got from the irrigation well to do dishes, baths, and wash clothes in. You could not drink the water; it had too much alkaline in it. We would have to haul drinking water from Uncle Paul's Farm, which was twenty-five miles away.

Mr. Corn owned this farm. His sister taught the fourth and fifth grades at Berrendo School. She was Mary Jo and my teacher when we first moved to New Mexico from Texas. Her name was Mrs. Smith and she was till teaching the same grades at that time.

Dad was still growing cotton and we were working in the fields in the summer chopping the weeds out of the cotton. The boys were plowing and helping Dad irrigate the cotton. We picked cotton in the fall until frost and after frost we were pulling bolls. We were still working in a field separate from the Mexicans.

Mom received blue chip or green stamps when she bought groceries. The drug store or some of the service stations would give green stamps. You would receive at least one stamp for every ten cents you spent. You would have to save up the stamps all year to get enough to fill the small book of fifty pages, unless you bought a lot of groceries, which we did. Mom spent $40.00 a week for groceries for a family of eight. That was a grocery cart full with no room to put any thing else in the cart. She bought a 50 pound bag of flour, 25 pound bag of potatoes, and 5 pound bags of different kinds of beans a week.

I would faithfully save the stamps until I could fill up four or five books It was a real treat to take the book of stamps to the blue chip or green stamp stores and pick out an item I was saving for. One time I picked out a pretty lamp and brought it home.   I loved lamps and still do.   Mom had a library table which I set the lamp on. I would do my home work there. I made the mistake of putting the lamp on an end table that Ray had made in wood shop at school. I would complain if Mary Jo or Annie got too close to the lamp. I was afraid they would break it. Mom did not have very many nice or pretty things, only the lamp and a few dishes.

One day Mary Jo was taking a nap. Mom called her to come to the kitchen to help her. She jumped up, went to the kitchen, bumped the table, and the lamp fell to the floor breaking into a hundred pieces. I was so upset I was fit to be tied. She did the very thing I knew she would do. I continued to save the stamps and got another lamp that was not as pretty.

Mary Jo and I would have chores we had to do daily.   One of the jobs she would have to do was help Mom in the kitchen.   I would have to make up beds, sweep and mop the floors, and we both had to do the laundry once a week. One of us would have to stay home each week to do the laundry in the ringer washer machine. My teacher wanted to know why I had to do the laundry every other week. I had to tell her, "Mom was always sick or having surgery and couldn't do the laundry." Mom went to the doctor once a week or once a month all my life up to that time.

We were at school one day when a snow storm hit in the afternoon before school let out for the day. That day I wore a light jacket with three quarters length sleeves to the elbow.   It was not cold when I left for school that morning. The bus dropped us off about half a mile from the house. Thank God, Dad was there to pick us up. I was so cold I couldn't feel my feet. That year was a very cold winter. It snowed a couple of times. The bus couldn't pick up anybody who was not within walking distance to State Road 285. The bus would not go down the country roads, which was not paved, after a snow storm.

Richard was a senior in high school. He hooked a cotton trailer to the tractor, and we would all ride on the trailer, the five miles to the State Road 285 to catch the bus. The tractor and trailer was left there and we would ride home on it after school. We did that every day until the snow melted and the dirt road was passable for vehicles.

That summer Ray was plowing the cotton field one day, the same field Mary Jo and I would be chopping the weeds out of the cotton the next day. Dad was out there working and Ray called to him to go and get the gun.   There was a very large rattle snake lying in the middle of the row that he was plowing. Dad ran to the house, got the gun, ran back out to the field, and shot the snake. Dad brought the dead rattle snake back to the yard. That was the largest rattle snake I had ever seen.   It was ten to twelve feet long, had ten rattlers, and a button.   It looked as large around

as a fence post and the head was as big as Dad's hand in length. The snake had been living on rabbits. A few days later, Mary Jo was going to get a bucket of water from the water pump. She was prancing by the chicken house (when she walked she would prance and skip). The chickens were squawking and flapping their wings and she looked up and saw a large snake slithering into the chicken house. She dropped the bucket and ran to get Dad. He had just come in from the field for the day. He got the gun and ran out to the chicken house. The snake was coiled and ready to strike. Dad did not flinch. He aimed the gun and shot the snake in the head before it could strike him. Dad was good with a gun; he could hit about anything that he aimed at.

The farm was surrounded by desert land and small hills with caves. There were a lot of rattle snakes out there. We walked up the hills to get to the field we would be working in that day. We stayed away from the caves. A couple of men who owned a restaurant in El Paso, Texas, which was over 200 miles away, drove down to the farm and hunted and killed the snakes. They served snake meat in their restaurant.

Some of the farmers that ranched or farmed out there did kill and eat rattle snake. They offered Dad some of the rattle snake meat and he declined. We did not ever eat rattle snake or jack rabbits killed on the land. We were poor but never went hungry.

Richard graduated from high school in May of 1956. He rented a room in town and went to work for the Coke Cola Bottling Co., driving a truck and delivering to the different stores. He bought himself a car to get back and forth to work, to go out to the farm on week ends, and to go any where else he wanted to.

Grandpa Zedlitz died that year and Dad went to East Texas with Aunt Ella and Uncle Paul to the funeral. We could not go because the work on the farm had to be done. I believe we were out of school for the summer.

Ray was a sophomore in high school. He wanted to buy a car and he got a part time job at a grocery store. Richard was renting a room in a rooming house and Ray moved into the room with him. He did not want to work on the farm any more. He bought himself a 1957, two door, hard top, Chevrolet, which was yellow and white in color. Richard and Ray were no longer living at home.

Helen Zedlitz age 16 1959

CHAPTER 16

It was 1957 and JW had his own farm now that he was renting. He stilled lived at home with us. He planted his own cotton and had to irrigate it. There was an early freeze that year that killed the young cotton sprouts. JW lost all of his cotton. The insurance did not pay enough to cover all the expenses and start over.

He went to work at Roswell Fire Department. He worked one day on and one day off. He bought himself a different car. My three brothers rented an apartment and stayed there for a while. I would go there on week ends sometime and clean the apartment and one of them would bring me back to the farm on a Sunday.

Mary Jo and I had to help Dad on the farm that summer. I was fourteen years old and Mary Jo was twelve. Annie was eleven years old. She was having pleurisy pain and was no help at all. Mary Jo and I learned to drive a tractor and drive dad's old truck. We learned how to drive by driving back and forth to the field. Berrendo School was building a new school, my class of 1957 was the first class to graduate from the eight grade. We went to school in the building only two weeks before we graduated. Mom bought me a pretty dress to wear to graduation. Richard bought me a nice watch, the first one I had ever had in my life.

It was a Saturday afternoon and Richard, JW, and a friend Bill Miller came out to the farm to see us. Mom was hanging out clothes on the clothe's line. She saw a UFO setting in mid air 200 feet above the hills behind the house. She never heard it making a noise. She just looked up and it was there. It was silver in color and long and round in an oval shape. Mom ran into the house to tell somebody to come out and see it. JW, Richard, Bill Miller, and Mary Jo followed Mom out to

see it. The UFO was still setting there like it was watching them as they were watching it. Richard said he watched it for ten minutes and it just disappeared in to thin air. Mary Jo said she looked away and looked back a few minutes later and it was gone. Our nearest neighbor was a Mexican family and they lived about one mile away. No one else saw it. I don't know where I was, I guess over at a girl friend's house. She lived about five miles from us up closer to State Highway 285. Believe it or not, it really did happen. We had not heard of the Roswell Incident in 1947 where a UFO crashed, even though we lived there at the time 10 years before.

That summer Mary Jo and I had to learn how to irrigate the cotton. We both had a hard time lifting the metal plate to stop the water from flowing down the ditch bank and water going where you didn't want it to go. We would have to raise the metal plate over our head and throw it into the area you wanted to dam up. The water would flow down the rows of cotton you wanted to irrigate. I weighed about a hundred pounds, was tall and skinny, and I didn't have the strength, to lift the metal plate up over my head and dam up the area without some water seeping out. Mary Jo didn't either. She was shorter and weighed less than I. We helped Dad the best we could. He was glad to get what little help we could give him. He would pay Mary Jo and me, $15.00 a week to buy our school clothes and shoes. We would put the clothes on lay-away and get them out when we paid them off.

Dad took us to church at Salt Creek Baptist Church on Sundays. After church sometimes two ladies, who had girls about our ages, would take all of us girls to the movies on Sunday afternoons. After the movies we would go to the A and W Root Beer drive in and get an orange or root beer float. They did take us home afterwards. What a delightful treat that was to us, since we only went to church on Sundays, worked five days, and to town on Saturdays. It cost $.50 each to go to the movies and maybe $.20 each for the orange or root beer float. I always got the orange float since it was my favorite.

One day that summer Mary Jo and I were standing in the yard and two deer came walking up. They were not afraid. I got some oats and one ate out of my hand. They must have been somebody's pets. JW ran an article in the lost and found in the Roswell's Daily Facts. No one responded to the article.

Mr. Corn, the land lord, had the deer picked up and placed in a petting zoo located next door to the City Park. The park had a lion in a cage without a tail. Two airmen decided to have some fun one night. They cut the lion's tail off. The news came out in the newspaper, on the radio, and on our one TV Channel. Years later I was living in California and ran across a man who had been stationed in Roswell, New Mexico at Walker Air Force Base at the time and was one of the culprits who cut that poor lions tail off. He still thought it was funny.

One Sunday that summer the members of the church decided to have a picnic in the mountains, which was 70 miles away. When we got there the pastor and all the young people that wanted to decided to walk up the mountain. Every one was supposed to stay together. We made it half way up and everybody was ready to walk back down. On the way down Mary Jo and Bobby Sperling decided to run down the mountain and be the first ones back to camp. After we all reached camp, Bobby was there but there was no sign of Mary Jo. We all called her name and honked the horns of the cars.

She was following Bobby but lost sight of him in the trees. She ran until she came to a road. She claimed she did not hear us calling and honking horns. She followed the road and it led her back to camp. We were all standing around wondering what to do and she came running up the road. She told us she was afraid of seeing a moose. There was no moose within a thousand miles. She could have seen a deer or two.

In August of 1957; I started to school at North Junior High School and was a freshman. I had a best friend that I had met in the lunch room. Her name was Sue Morrison and she was in the eight grade. We had a lot fun that year. I spent a lot of week ends with her. We would go to her Grandpa's house or her Uncle Buster and Aunt's Kakie's house, to baby sit their three children, or at her Mom and Dad's house.

I had my first boy-friend during that time for about three months. He never wanted to go any where and he had a car. He would get upset even though he didn't want to go if Sue and I went to the movies once in a while on a Saturday afternoon. We even saw the movie I want to live, where Rita Haywood star as a woman executed in the electric chair. All he wanted to do was sit around the house and watch TV. I finally broke up with him.

JW bought a trailer house and he, and the two boys lived there. Richard changed jobs and was not in town every day. JW was still working at the Fire Department every other day. Ray was a junior in high school and still worked part time. He was working at the cemetery digging graves and watering the grass on the graves until midnight every night.

Mary Jo and I took turns staying Saturday night in the trailer house cleaning it and one of the brothers would bring us back to the farm on Sunday.

It was in the fall of 1957, on Saturday Dad, Mom, and I drove to town in Dad's GMC pickup truck. Mary Jo and Annie decided to stay home since we were only going to town to get groceries and right back home. A storm was suppose to be coming and snow was predicted.

On the way to town Dad had trouble keeping the truck running. He had to stop and clean out the filter which was clogging up.

When we arrived at the grocery store, we rushed around picking out what we would need for a week and paid for our groceries. We left the store and stopped by the trailer.

The snow was falling. So, Richard decided to take us home in his car since the groceries would get wet in the back of the truck.

His car had electric windows and all four windows was down. He pushed the button and nothing happened. The windows would not go up. He was going to have to get the windows fixed. On a Saturday afternoon it was impossible. So, Dad and Richard decided to drive the car out to the farm anyway. Richard drove half way and he turned around and drove back to the trailer. We were freezing to death.

We spent the night in the trailer house with the boys. JW was working at the Fire Department for twenty-four hours. Ray arrived later. He was working at the cemetery digging graves.

We got up and left early the next morning in the GMC pickup truck. It had stopped snowing and the road was clear. We made it home without any trouble.

When we got home Mary Jo and Annie were hungry but alright. Mom and Dad worried about them. They said they had split one boiled egg the day before and that was all that they had to eat. They spent most of the day in bed to keep warm watching TV.

The gas range was all we had to keep the two rooms warm. The burners on top of the stove and the oven. The oven had to be lit with a match. Mary Jo was afraid to light the oven. When you turned on the gas to the oven the match had better be lit next to the jet or it would blow you across the room. I know that happened to me once and made a believer of me.

Ray Zedlitz age 15, 1953

CHAPTER 17

It was 1958. Dad gave up on farming that year. The boys went on to new jobs and new lives. There were only us three skinny girls to help him. We did not have the time, endurance or stamina to work that hard and work in the house too.

Dad went to work running his own service station in Lake Arthur, New Mexico. It was located south of Roswell, New Mexico on State Highway 285. It was a small village with maybe 50 people. A lot of travelers went through there and Dad made most of his money from the travelers. It had a house next door to live in, with a bathroom, piped in water, and electricity. You may wonder why I stress so much on a house which we lived in having the luxuries of electricity, piped in water and a bathroom. Until you have had to live without these luxuries most of your life, you could not understand how a person could feel.

Mary Jo and Annie went to Lake Arthur with Dad to live. Mom found a live-in job in Roswell, baby sitting, cleaning, and cooking. I was still a freshman in junior high school. I stayed with the boys and went to school, cooked when there was food, cleaned the trailer, and washed clothes at the laundromat. Mary Jo stayed three months in Lake Arthur with Dad and came back to Roswell and stayed in the trailer with me. We both slept on the couch that made into a bed. She went to North Junior High with me, since she was in the seventh grade. Ray drove us to school every morning the rest of the school year. He graduated in May of that year.

We had a friend who lived next door. He was working for the 7 Up Bottling Company driving a truck delivering the bottles of soda out of town. That summer of 1958, he hired Mary Jo as a helper. She was only twelve years old but spent the summer working with him. She sorted the empty bottles and put them in the case of 24. The company bottled not only 7 up, but Mission

orange, grape, strawberry, and root beer. They had to be sorted into cases of each brand of soda. When they returned at the end of the day those cases would be unloaded and ready to go through the machine to wash the bottles and refill for distribution. She bought her own clothes that summer. I did not have a job and I did not have any money to buy any new clothes. We both had to wear each others clothe's that school year.

After graduation Ray got a job driving a truck delivering gas to the service stations. We did not see to much of him after that. He was in and out and he did sleep in the trailer at night. Richard would come home on the weekends, since he worked out of town all week. JW still worked one day on and one day off. I found out later on the days he was off, he would go to Lake Arthur and cook Dad and Annie a good meal. He would come back to the trailer to sleep at night. The only food we saw JW buy was when he would send Mary Jo to the store to get him a TV dinner or a bag of bananas. He would sit there and eat in front of us. He would send me to the store until I got wise and made sure I was not around. I spent a lot of time on week ends over at Sue's and her family's. I did ride home with her on the school bus on a Friday and somebody would take me home on a Sunday or I would spend a few days if it was in the summer.

When Richard came back to town on the week ends, he would buy groceries, and I would go with him and help buy food to cook. I was taking home economics and learning how to sew and cook. I did cook when there was food. JW and Ray were usually there to eat if JW was not working. There were times when I only had a dime to buy a donut. If they had any day old donuts, I could get one for a nickel for supper from the bakery next door to the trailer park.

Dad would give us our lunch money every week and I would eat my lunch at school. They had good lunches back then. Mary Jo would go with a friend, Janey, and they would buy a package of potato chips and a coke for their lunch. She saved the rest to buy a dress or something she needed.

Mary Jo would eat either a cheese sandwich or a bowl of cornflakes for supper. One reason why was Richard did not eat meat and would not buy it. The reason I did not eat the cheese or cornflakes for supper was I don't remember them. Maybe because I had not eaten cheese since I was about eight years old and got sick at my stomach and the last thing I had eaten was a cheese sandwich and a package of Frito's. I never ate cheese and Frito again for years. As for the cornflakes, I did not like them, did not eat them for years, In fact, 50 years passed before I tried another bowl of cornflakes. I have been told that I was not there and must have been out at Sue's house.

Mary Jo and I never asked Dad for any extra money for food. I don't know why but we didn't. In fact we never talked about anything that bothered us. We never had anybody we could trust enough to go to. If we went to Mom, she would just ignore the situation and act like everything was fine. She never offered us any money from what she made either. Annie asked her; "Mom I need some money to buy some school clothes?" Mom answered her, "It is not my responsibility to buy your school clothes, go and ask your Dad for the money."

JW hurt his back at the Fire Department and had to have surgery. He recuperated in the trailer. He was in bed for three months and expected us to wait on him hand and foot and we did. He had to learn how to walk again. He practiced walking on crutches from one end of the trailer to the other end. He had a girlfriend, Betty Chumley, she would come over and visit with him when she was not working. She had been married before and had two small children. They planned on getting married when he get well enough to go back to work.

While JW was recovering from surgery on his back I noticed a scar on his leg. I ask him, "How did you get that scar on your leg?" He told me, "Do you remember when I was in Korea and I was suppose to come home on leave and didn't because I wrote and told you all I was in the hospital having surgery for hemorrhoids. Actually we had gone on a mission and I was shot in the leg and had surgery on my leg to remove the bullet." While he was in the hospital his squadron had been attacked and were all killed. When he got out of the hospital he was sent back home to the United States. That was the only time I ever heard him talk about the war. So I don't know the complete story, he did not want Mom to ever know.

That summer I was 16 years old and could get a job. I went to work at the 7 up Bottling Plant. I sorted the different types of soda bottles in case of 24 bottles. I helped stack the cases on pallets higher than my head. One of the boys drove a fork lift to pick up the pallets of cases of empty bottles to carry over to the conveyed belt. Another person put each case on the belt, which would carry the cases to another person, who put the empty bottles in the machine to be washed. Once the bottles were washed, the belt would bring the bottles around to be inspected for breakage, and dirty bottles, which I would remove from the belt. The bottles continued on the belt to a machine which filled the bottles with soda, cap the bottles, and moved on to be set in a case of 6 or 24 by another machine. A person was at the end of the line, stacking the cases on a pallet, which would be moved with the forklift to another part of the building and stored. The truck drivers would get their orders filled from the stock pile of pallets of sodas.

I worked all that summer to buy my sisters and I clothes or material I could make our dresses with. I even bought a Singer Sewing Machine. That August I was a junior in high school. I took my second year of home economics. I practiced cooking new dishes on the family. They always ate it all so I guess it was good. I entered a cooking contest and won third place. My cake had two layers and one dropped in the middle. The teacher had me put the layer that had dropped in the middle, upside down on the plate, and place the other layer on top. I cooked the pineapples with corn starch to thicken the juice and placed it in the middle and in a circle in the center of the top layer of the cake. I made a frosting of egg whites mixed in corn syrup and vanilla flavoring and put around the circle of crushed pineapples, in the middle of the top layer, and on the side of the cake. It turned out to be a very pretty cake. I had to get Richard to come to the school and pick up the cake one morning. I spent the day at school and planned on having a slice of the cake when I got home. Wrong, the all of the cake had been eaten. I did not even get a taste of it. The family told me it was good.

JW went back to work at the Fire Department. He and Betty got married. He sold the trailer and moved to a house across the street from his in-laws. We had to move again. Richard rented a house right next door to JW and Betty. Some of Mom's furniture was moved into the house. The rest Dad was using in Lake Arthur. I know the piano was down there. There were at least two beds that Dad and Annie used. Both houses were fully furnished. Dad had the furniture stored out at Uncle Paul's farm. Aunt Ella made him pay storage fees for the two years the furniture was stored.

Dad gave us money for groceries and lunch money for school every week. Mom baby sat

Betty's two children while she worked. Her son, Darvon, was 5 years old and her daughter, Karen, was 6 years old and going to school. I took in ironing from the neighbors and finished paying for my Singer Sewing Machine. The husband to the lady next door was in the Air Force and worked in the mess hall cooking. He wore starched white clothes. She washed and starched them and I ironed them. I could iron them like he wanted them, like they had been ironed in a cleaners. I ironed that whole year for them.

One night Mom and I went over to see Sue Morrison and her Mom. They was living in a trailer house north of Roswell near Walker Air Force Base. There was a family next door the Morrisons' were friends with. The guy was in the Air Force.

That night while we were there the lady ran over to Sue's house screaming that her husband had shot her three year old son. He was right behind her carrying a rifle on his shoulder and screamed at her to get outside he was going to shoot her. The woman hid behind Mom and had her scared to death.

Sue and I slipped out the door and I went over to the house to see if he really had shot the little boy. The child was laying face down on the floor, with blood coming out a bullet hole on his left side and just below his shoulder blade.

I knelt down on the floor to see the child and the man still had the gun on his shoulder. He told me, "Don't touch him, an ambulance will be coming." I didn't feel any fear of the man. He was drunk and very upset with his wife. He had calmed down and wasn't threatening in any way. It looked like when he got the gun, the child must have been in the way, when the gun accidentally discharged.

I went back outside, the ambulance had arrived, and I didn't want to be in the way. They went into the house and placed the child on a stretcher. They put him in the ambulance. The wife came out still screaming at her husband and got into the ambulance with her son. They took off with sirens blaring to the base hospital.

The cops finally arrived and talked to the man, put him in hand cuffs, and carried him off to jail. The couple had a small baby sleeping in the bedroom. I don't know what happened to the baby unless Sue's Mom kept her until her mother came home from the hospital. Mom had enough, so we left and went back to the house.

We found out later that the bullet went through the child's lung and came out through his back. The child had surgery and was going to be fine.

We found out that the husband got drunk, came home, and started a fight with his wife. He had found out that she had been having an affair with one of his friends. He had gone into the bedroom, got the gun, and threaten to shoot his wife. The child was standing there when the gun went off. He didn't intend to shoot the child, that was an accident. I don't know how the gun discharged accidentally unless he was too drunk to aim the gun.

The District Attorney subpoenaed Mom and me to come to the court house and make a statement of what we saw. I was sixteen years old. He took my statement, but Mom had to appear as a witness. I told them basically the same thing that I have related at this writing.

He got off with time served in jail. The wife left and took the children and went back to Texas, where she was from. We met the man later and he thanked Mom and me for helping him get out of jail.

CHAPTER 18

It was 1959. Dad had to give up the service station in Lake Arthur. He left the piano in the house when he moved to Artesia, a larger town about 15 miles from Lake Arthur. State Highway 285 was being rerouted and a new double lane road was put in going to Artesia, which by passed Lake Arthur.

Dad opened up another service station in Artesia. Annie came back to Roswell to live. She was in the sixth grade. Dad rented a one bed room house to live in. Richard, Mom, and the girl were driving to Artesia to see Dad. Richard, Mom and Mary Jo were sitting in the front seat. Annie was sitting in the back seat. When they get to the city limits a car crossed the road in front of them. Richard saw the car, slowed down, and could not avoid hitting the other car. His car spins around one full circle, the door on the passenger side came open, and Mary Jo was hanging on for dear life. The other car spins around a couple of times and turned over on its side.

Someone called the police and an ambulance arrived and took all of them to the hospital. Richard hurt his back and wore a cast for three months. Mom had a punctured lung, had surgery, and spent two weeks in the hospital in Artesia. Annie had a whiplash and Mary Jo had a few scratches. The police took Richard, Mary Jo and Annie over to see Dad at his service station to let him know what had happened. They stayed a few hours with Dad, called the Sheriff's Office when they were ready to go home and the Sheriff drove them back to Roswell, which was 40 miles from Artesia.

Mom was not released at the end of the two weeks. She was transferred to Saint Mary Hospital in Roswell to be closer to the family. Richard was unable to work the three month he was in a cast.

He filed a law suit against the driver of the other car. They eventually received a settlement. The amount was unknown. Richard and Mom received the settlement and they never said how much the settlement was. Mary Jo and Annie received $15.00 each.

While Richard was off work he drove Annie to school every day. She was in the sixth grade. Richard had a 1959 green Chevrolet car he drove the first day. The next time he took Annie to school he drove Ray's 1959 dark blue Chevrolet Impala. Ray was having some car trouble and used another red car as a loner, while his was being fixed. Richard drove Annie to school in the red car also.

A boy in her class noticed Annie coming to school in different colored cars. His curiosity got the best of him, he would wait every day for her just to see what color of car she would be in. One day he finally ask Annie, "How many cars do you have?" Annie answered him in jest, " I just push a button and the car changes color." The boy said, "I sure wish we had a car like that." Annie never told him the truth. That summer I worked at the 7 Up Bottling Company again. I did basically the same thing I did the summer before. I usually had to walk back to the house and it was about 2 miles from the company where I was working. A Mexican lady I worked with would give me a ride home after work sometimes. She was married and had two small children. Her mother took care of the children when she worked. We would sometimes stop at her mother's house and she would have lunch ready. She was a good cook and made the best tacos. I had never seen or eaten a taco before. They had to show me how to fix it. She had also made a bowl of green jell-o with crushed pineapples in it that was so good. That was another first time for me.

The first time I had a chance to get the ingredients, I made the tacos and they were a success, because the boys had not ever eaten them before either. Mom only cooked the basic southern foods and never in variation. My mind was like a sponge, I would remember anything I really liked and would go home and try to make it.

A few weeks later I made a bowl of green jell-o with crushed pineapples and went to work. I was planning on having a bowl when I got home after work. I worked five or six hours and walked home. When I walked in the house, I saw the bowl in the sink. It was empty and not a person was around. I was so aggravated that I just sat down and cried. I could not make any more because I had used all the jell-o and crushed pineapple on hand, and I was too tired to walk to the store to buy some more.

If I cooked something, I would have to stay there and guard it. If I wanted to eat any of it, other wise, I would not get even a taste of it. I bought a Betty Crocker Cooked Book, while I was taking home economics, and I was trying a lot of different dishes we had never eaten before. In fact, the recipe for the cake I made in the cooking contest came from that same cook book. I still had the cook book at the time of this writing.

Mom would make jell-o plain or full of canned peaches. She would say it was because Richard liked it that way. If she made a pie, it would be what Richard was supposed to have liked. If she bought cereal it was what Richard liked. The trouble was I found out Richard did not even know he liked these foods so much. That was Mom's way of not buying a lot of different things the rest of liked because she didn't have enough money to buy them. She just bought what she liked and let us think Richard was getting everything he loved to eat.

CHAPTER 19

John Fitzgerald Kennedy announced his candidacy in January, 1960, and set out to demonstrate that a Catholic could be elected and that his youth was no handicap. He ran against Republican Vice President Richard M. Nixon.

It was March, 1960, and I had my eighteenth birthday. I was finishing up my junior year. I hoped the rest of that year would be uneventful. Annie was in the eight grade at South Junior High. We moved again, this time to the house on Sunset Avenue in Roswell. Ray opened up a Chevron Service Station. He wanted Dad to give up the station in Artesia and work for him.

Mom started baby sitting. She was getting more and more children to keep while their mother's worked. Richard put a chain link fence around the house. The City of Roswell found out that she did not have a license to baby sit that many children and closed her down. The guide lines that Mom would have to follow in fixing the house to their specifications would cost too much. She could baby sit three children without a license. She did baby sit three babies for a while. Two of the babies' daddy's were friends of Ray.

Ray was having trouble with the gas and money not matching up. His so called friends were taking gas and not paying for it. Chevron wanted Ray to let Dad go because he was over 60 years old. Dad did not even have a vehicle to put gas in. I do not know what really happened there.

Dad had to find another job. He found a job driving a school bus and Mom would cook in the cafeteria with Mary Jo's help. She was a freshman in junior high and quit school The job was in Penasko, New Mexico and they would have to drive a hundred miles to get there. They would come back home on week ends. They drove Ray's company truck while they were working down there. They stayed in a furnished trailer on one of the rancher's land during the week. Dad worked three or four months and it snowed. Dad would have trouble starting the bus every morning when it was cold. That morning it did not start at all. The truck would not start either. Dad could not go to pick up the children to take to school. Mom could not get to the school to cook lunch in the cafeteria.

The principal was a teacher too. He did both jobs. The School of Penasko and a couple of houses were all that was there. It was a small school grades first through eighth grades located in the hilly country side and surrendered by ranch land. Artesia was the nearest town. One boy went to high school there. Dad had to pick him up at the bus stop and take him home to the ranch next to where Dad, Mom and Mary stayed.

The principal was so mad that he fired Mom for not coming to work, even though the bus and truck would not start. He could not fire Dad. The two jobs went together; they only made a $100.00 each in a month. Dad got mad because he had to quit because the principal had fired Mom, and he hit the principal in the nose knocking him to the floor. Dad, Mom, and Mary Jo went back home to the house on Sunset.

Dad got a job for a few weeks working as a helper picking up garbage. That was during the month of December. He got another job working for his nephew, Lloyd King, on the Clarity's farm. He would be irrigating cotton. There was a three room house for him to live in.

CHAPTER 20

On January 20, 1961, John Fitzgerald Kennedy was inaugurated as president. In his inaugural address, he said that leadership had passed to a new generation of Americans. He summoned his listeners and so, my fellow Americans, ask not what your country can do for you: ask what you can do for your country. My fellow citizens of the world: ask not what America will do for you, but what together we can do for the freedom of man. Shortly after he took office. President Kennedy set the goal of placing a man on the moon by the end of the 1960's.

I was a senior in high school and I had finally made it. Annie was in the ninth grade still going to South Junior High School. She was walking to school one day when a car pulled up to the curb and stopped. The driver slid over to the passenger's side, rolled down the window, and said, "Little girl do you need a ride," Annie answered, "No". Our dog named Sparky was following her to school. He growled at the man. The man slid back over to the driver's side and took off like a bat out of hell. We had never heard of pedophile or even knew what it meant. We were born poor and we had a sheltered life. If we didn't hear it at school or church or we did not read about it, we never heard of it. Mom or Dad never talked to us about any thing that we might need to know. We did not ever talk to each other about anything that happened to us. We kept it to ourselves.

Sparky continued to follow Annie to school and stayed with her all day. Once he knew where her classes were upstairs or downstairs, he would beat her there and crawl under her desk. If the door wasn't open, he would wait for her. In fact, he was the first one there every

day. Annie's first class for the day was art. One day a student didn't come to class. Her stool was empty. Sparky jumped upon her stool, put his paws on the table, and looked at the teacher as though he was ready to go to work. The teacher and the whole class roared with laughter. The art teacher asked, "Who does this dog belong to?" A class mate spoke up and said, "He follows Annie to school every day." The teacher told the class, "This dog should be a good example to you all. He is always on time, never missed a day, and doesn't continually interrupt the class."

On Fridays, Sparky followed Annie to the Assembly Hall and sat in a chair next to her. After the Assembly meeting , one day the art teacher told a boy in the class to put the dog outside. A door from the art class did lead out side. The boy picked Sparky up, took him to the door, bent down to let him out, and before he raised back up, Sparky was back in the room. The teacher must have called the dog pound because they came and picked him up at school. Annie told Richard and Ray about Sparky being picked up by the dog pound for going to school. They just laughed and did not go and get him. We never saw Sparky again.

One night Mary Jo and Annie were at home alone. A neighbor lady and her daughter came over to the house. Someone knocked on the back door. Annie and the little girl went to the door and opened it. All she was able to see was black. Someone dressed in all black from head to foot said, "This is a hold up," and put a gun in her face. The little girl and Annie started screaming and running into the living room where Mary Jo and the neighbor were sitting on the sofa. They asked, "What happened?" Annie cried, "Run." Annie was in a state of panic and they all ran around the coffee table a couple of times trying to figure out what direction to go. One of them saw the front door and said, "Lets' go out the front door." They ran out the front door, around the back of the house, to the neighbors house still screaming. The neighbor's husband came out to see what the screaming was about. After they told him, he called the police. The police came out and Annie gave the description of a person dressed from head to foot in black. She didn't even know if it was a real gun. The police asked the little girl for a description and she said, "The burglar was dressed in polka dot shirt and pants." Annie said, "He was not, the person was dressed in all black." The little girl was so frighten she was seeing polka dots. The police checked out the house and yard. The gate was wide open. The burglar didn't take time to close it. One of the police said, "I saw someone dressed in all black running down the street, and there was no grass growing under his feet." I don't know who was the most frightened, Annie or the burglar. I would call that the bungled holdup.

The house on Sunset Avenue had some strange things happen there to my sister and me. The first incident happened to Annie. She was in the bathroom sitting on the toilet with her clothes down around her ankles. We always locked the door after we went in the bathroom. If we didn't, somebody would always walk in on you. She said, "The door was locked," and I believed her. While she was in there the door did fly open and slammed against the wall with a bang. She jumped up, finished dressing, and stormed into the kitchen accusing Mary Jo of pushing the bathroom door open.

Mary Jo looked at Annie like she was crazy. She and Mom had been cooking in the kitchen and had not left the room. There was not anybody else in the house but them. I was baby siting

two children down the street from the house.

Then it happened to Mary Jo a couple of times, the same way, and once when she was getting into the bathtub. The locked door flew open and slammed against the wall with such force that it shook the house.

One day I stayed home from school sick. I knew I was alone in the house. I decided to take a hot bath thinking it would make me feel better. It was a bright sunny day and no reason to feel any apprehension. I went into the bathroom and locked the door ever though I was alone. I didn't want someone coming into the house while I was bathing. I took all my clothes off, and while I was doing that I heard the back door open, foot steps stomping through the kitchen and down the hall toward the bathroom. There was another small hallway leading to the back bedroom and you would have to pass right by the bathroom door. I was thinking Ray must have forgotten something and come back to get it. He still had the service station at that time. I got into the bath water, sit down in the tub and the door flew open and slammed against the wall with a bang. No one was standing in the door way. I about broke my neck getting out of the tub and getting some clothes on. I searched every room, closets and even under the beds and nobody was in the house but me.

May 6, 1961, the United States sent its first man into space, Alan B. Shepherd, Jr. He made a suborbital flight, becoming the first American in space.

Graduation was coming up. I did not attend graduation but I did receive a high school diploma. I have come down the long, hard, and rocky road of life. The future was before me, holding new promises, experiences, changes, and hardships. I embraced the future with a loving heart and open arms.

ON WINGS MORE DELICATE
By James D. Freeman

> *The butterflies go fluttering by.*
> *How do they know that they can fly?*
> *Had we been only crawling things,*
> *Would we know what to do with wings?*
> *I wonder. Still I think we might,*
> *For we too have hopes of flight,*
> *Through of a different kind,*
> *Since ours is mainly in our mind.*
> *We have to trust ourselves on less,*
> *Than even air or emptiness.*
> *On wings more delicately wrought,*
> *Than butterflies'--mere wings*
> *of thought-*
> *But oh, sometimes with what surprise,*
> *How exquisite high we rise!*

Helen Zedlitz
October, Senior picture, 1960